PRAISE FOR MICHAEL STRASNER AND MASTERING LEADERSHIP

"The difference Michael Strasner has made in my life is monumental in that he was one of the first people to give me feedback around community and what was actually possible in my leadership. He showed me that I was playing the game unconsciously and thinking there was only so much energy to go around. I was keeping people at arm's distance who were close to me and making it more about the mission and 'saving' the world but missing that the world was right there in front of me and with me every single day in the trenches."

— Preston Smiles, best-selling author of *LOVE LOUDER*

Michael is a master leader and working with him has taught me to see things differently, through a clearer lens. I've learned to communicate with intention, to create deeper relationships with others, to examine my own patterns in what's holding me back. Choosing to stand up in The Drift and show people what it means to go all in and change the world makes for a more fulfilling life for all of us.

— Natalie Jill, Natalie Jill Fitness

Michael Strasner is a master coach and facilitator, Jedi of transformation, and leader of leaders. As a podcaster, speaker & coach, I've had the good fortune of learning from Michael and practicing his signature leadership distinctions over the last five years, which has helped me clarify my vision, smoothly navigate challenges, and maximize my impact on others. If you're looking for tangible tools that will support you in being a leader in life and work, Michael's books will be a staple in your toolbox.

-- Mark Shapiro, TEDx: The Art of Authentic Connection In A Digital World

Michael, I want to acknowledge you because you are a blessing and inspiration to this world. You inspired me to open my heart to be a vulnerable, loving and connected man. You are a great leader and an amazing mentor. The way you support people in this world by living the distinctions of leadership is unprecedented. What a blessing your book is going to be for every reader.

— Alex Arriaga, co-Founder of Kensington Investment Fund

PRAISE FOR MICHAEL STRASNER AND MASTERING LEADERSHIP

As an engineer and former military officer, I spent most of my life learning to be analytical and logical. With Michael's coaching, I gained the tools to make choices based on who I say I am and how I want to live my life, guided not by the daily noise of life or the opinions of others, but rather by my most deeply held values to pursue life fully and freely. I founded a venture firm, co-created one of the world's best distilleries and fell in love with the most loving and generous woman I have ever known, creating a relationship that I always longed for but had never been able to obtain.
   – Dr. Wynn S. Sanders (Lt Colonel, USAF), Founder, Cambridge Street Ventures

Michael Strasner is magnetic. His vision of a world of leaders responsible for it all is not just something he preaches. He practices it with ferocious grace and creates environments where all in his presence can't help but transform. Michael leads from love and light ensuring that we all know the power we have to make a difference for everyone we touch. He is a true master, a leader of leaders with a mission to create more and transform the world. You will not be the same after you encounter him. Nor will the world, because he is responsible for it all!
   – Wendi McKenna, DPT, Founder of Move Play Grow

It is with great pleasure that I recommend *Mastering Leadership* to all who seek massive results and the desire to live an extraordinary life. Michael is the quintessential example of integrity, purpose, vision, and commitment and he has inspired countless people who have a thirst for becoming leaders and creating tremendous results in their lives. I am thrilled for all who read this book. To have the opportunity to see the world through Michael's lens has personally inspired me to live a more loving, abundant, and results-driven life, or as Michael says: "a life worth living."
   – Todd J. Weinstein, Esq. Del Shaw Moonves Tanaka Finkelstein & Lezcano

PRAISE FOR LIVING ON THE SKINNY BRANCHES

"*Living on the Skinny Branches* is an opportunity to rediscover the joy and passion of your youth by taking courageous action now to transform your life and the world around you."

–Brad Blanton, Ph.D., author of *Radical Honesty*

"Michael creates champions in business and life. In almost 30 years, he has brought passion, infectious enthusiasm humor and commitment to making a difference in others. A devoted father and husband, Michael gives 150% to everyone. Let Michael bring out the champion in you as you make your way to the Skinny Branches of your life."

– Beth Hollahan, Owner and Managing Director, MEH Consulting Group

"When I looked to enroll in training to enhance my leadership skills, I didn't want just another motivational trainer. I wanted someone that could help me with tools to unlock my potential, ignite my passion, and to realize my own vision for my personal and professional life. Michael Strasner quickly proved that he was that person. He helped illuminate the path to discover my own inner strengths and to leave my comfort zone to see the leader I am capable of being. With his caring, compassionate, and authentic approach he has provided the guidance that is allowing me to transform and realize the life I truly want to live."

—Wayne Carlson, former Professor of Design, Vice Provost for Undergraduate Studies, Dean of Undergraduate Education, The Ohio State University

"Michael Strasner is truly a world class coach, trainer, and leader. His ability to 'read' someone and communicate his perception on how that person "is showing up" to others is unrivaled by anyone I have met in my 25+ year career. He challenges people to consider new possibilities in their lives and in doing so creates the opportunity for people to close the gap between their potential and their achievement. I am truly grateful for the contributions he has made to my businesses and my life."

– Jeff Kaye, Co-CEO, Kaye/Bassman International Corp

MASTERING LEADERSHIP

SHIFT THE DRIFT AND CHANGE THE WORLD

Michael Strasner

"A life is not important except
in the impact it has on other lives."
- Jackie Robinson

DEDICATION

"My student and now friend Tracy Austin died this morning. I am and will forever be empowered by how he lived, and by who he was for his family, friends, co-workers, the community and the world. Tracy, the torch you carried was a beacon of infinite light, grace, humility, passion, courage, love, and vision that will forever transcend your time here on earth. Even your laugh was amazing and outrageous. Fly with the angels, my brother. It should be easy, you always have. With all my love, Michael."

The above is from a Facebook post Michael Strasner wrote about my husband Tracy on June 27, 2017. Tracy completed Michael's four-day Breakthrough training workshop in Columbus, Ohio in October 2016.

Tracy was an educator, coach, and an enthusiastic student of leadership. He was well known and greatly loved for his positive attitude, kindness, and brilliant smile. Even so, Michael Strasner's leadership and ways of being blew him away. I believe Michael inspired in Tracy a vision that none of us could have imagined then—what Michael calls an "unimaginable life."

A few days after that pre-Halloween workshop, we learned Tracy had stage four pancreatic cancer. His prognosis: dead by Christmas.

Tracy opted for chemo to buy some more time, and on a cold, windy day in early November declared to me the vision that would lead the rest of his life: "I'm going to use my cancer for giving." For Giving.

And he did. Tracy gave the world—both in person and on social media—his vision of what dying looked like. He chose to rise above it, to use it to empower himself and everyone he encountered right up until his last breath. Instead of, "Why me?" Tracy asked, "Why not me?" And sometimes, even on his most painful days, said, "Watch me!"

Over the remaining months, Tracy inspired events, songs, and fundraising for other cancer patients. We transparently and comfortably talked publicly about death and sickness. Tracy gave speeches, won awards, connected strangers. And at his funeral, hundreds of people—previously known only to each other on social media—met in person.

Michael visited Tracy in hospice three days before he died. My strapping husband was a skeleton of himself by then; his voice and energy almost gone. When Michael walked into Tracy's line of sight, he smiled, and his emaciated, once-strong arms floated slowly up for a hug. Michael sat down next to him and said, "Tracy I'm going to dedicate my next book to you," and that was the last thing I heard.

In that darkened hospice room on a sunny summer morning in June, Michael put his lips to Tracy's ear and coached him. Tracy listened, and whispered, and nodded. Only they know what passed between them.

What I saw pass between them, and what I will remember until MY last breath, is leadership. I can still see those two heads so close together—Michael, who's spent his life transforming other lives and Tracy, who used his death to do the same. I can still hear their quiet murmurs—two master leaders concluding their earthly business together.

In one four-day workshop, Michael Strasner passed the light of leadership to Tracy and evoked in him the possibility of creating a life and vision that was unprecedented and unimaginable. And in the next eight months—even as death became his unprecedented and unimaginable future—Tracy passed that light to others.

Together, Michael and Tracy created a shared vision that I now embody as my own, and that all of us can choose. Life is now.

No matter what life hands us—even if it's our mortality—it also hands us the opportunity to lead, to choose to step into the unknown, to create with gusto what Michael calls "something that wasn't going to happen anyway."

It's the way all of us—collectively—will change the world.

—Karen Austin

FOREWARD

Dear Reader,

I wanted to start this off by saying thank you so much for choosing to read my father's newest book, *Mastering Leadership: Shift the Drift and Change the World*. It is a humbling honor and privilege to write this foreword on behalf of my siblings and me, and I'm ecstatic to have the opportunity to express our love, appreciation, admiration, and respect for our father, Michael Strasner.

Ever since I was little, I've known that I do not have a "normal" father with a "normal" job. I have been asked many times throughout my life what my dad does for work, and, to be honest, that question rarely comes with an easy, straightforward answer. Usually, I attempt to define what he does as simply as I can, but I've always found it incredibly difficult to summarize my father's work in just a few words.

Yes, he absolutely is a leadership trainer/coach by definition, but, to us, he is the most devoted, selfless, supportive, and caring dad to all five of his children while also being a multifaceted trainer and coach who has dedicated his life to transforming the lives of hundreds of thousands of people around the world.

My dad is my hero, my role model, and everything that I aspire and strive to be. When I found out that this book is about mastering leadership, I was instantly excited by knowing that my dad will be sharing some of the wisdom that I have been fortunate enough to witness firsthand for 22 years.

My dad provides us with unconditional guidance and support, and I attribute most of who I am and how I present myself to the way he raised us. He has always gone beyond expectations to ensure that our family is cared for and supported both financially and emotionally, and he is truly the backbone of the Strasner family.

Thanks to my dad, I am courageous but careful, I am strong but soft, I am flexible but passionate, I am lighthearted but sincere, I am gentle but tough. He taught me about the history of the Boston Red Sox while braiding my hair, and I will be eternally grateful for the balance that he has instilled into my character and my life simply by being who he is. My dad has mastered the art of leading by example because his authentic, brave, and true self is a natural born leader.

I don't know anyone who works as hard and as passionately as my dad does, and I genuinely cannot remember the last time I've heard him complain or be anything but positive and driven. I believe that he is this way because he not only loves and lives for what he does, but he truly embodies everything that he teaches in his trainings, coaching, and seminars.

My dad created extraordinary results in his life through perpetual personal development, and it inspires us to have the strength to do the same for ourselves. Having my father to look up to and model my life after has been the greatest gift life can offer me, and each day I ask myself what I can do to express my gratitude and appreciation for his endless sacrifices and generosity to all of those around him. He motivates me to be the best version of myself that I can possibly be because I know he sees that within me and wants that person to shine through the exterior. My dad challenges me to work harder and never settle for less than what I deserve, and I don't know where I would be without him.

To say that I am proud of my father would be a serious understatement. I could not possibly have more pride and reverence for everything that he has accomplished and everything that he effortlessly conquers daily. I wish that every child could have a father like mine because he is everything that I love and cherish about myself. I know that I will raise my future children with somebody just like him someday, thanks to his showing me what I am worthy of as a woman and leader.

I started this foreword off by thanking you, the reader, for taking the time to read this book. I want to end this by thanking my father for being who he is.

Thank you, dad, for living your life with such purpose that it drives everyone around you to do the same for themselves. I live my life every day to prove to you that your hard work has all been worthwhile. Thank you for loving me, for pushing me. Thank you for being a man of your word. Thank you for guiding me. Thank you for being honest with me. Thank you for never settling. Thank you for living your life the way that you do.

I love you up to the sky and back, dad. You're our family's standard for all people.

Savannah Strasner
Student
Daughter of Michael Strasner
(along with Nick, Andrew, Haley, and Conner)

CONTENTS

PREFACE

Hello. My name is Michael Strasner. I am a master leader. Not because I know everything, far from it. I became a master leader as the result of practicing and rigorously applying the 12 Distinctions of Master Leaders (on which this book is based) in my professional and personal life. With commitment and tenacity, you also can become a master leader.

What does it mean to be a master leader? A master leader is a human being who makes a declaration to cause something and who then—through specific and distinct ways of being—takes committed, intentional action to make it happen. Master leaders cause the change they want to see in the world.

Who do you think of when you think of a leader? Martin Luther King, Jr.? Oprah? Theo Epstein? Perhaps Mandela. Jesus? Malala? Or maybe you think of Jaclyn Corin, David Hogg, Emma Gonzalez, Cameron Kasky, and Matt Deitsch, who are some of the inspirational young leaders from Marjory Stoneman Douglas High School in Parkland, Florida, who created the March for Our Lives movement and the Road to Change Tour to register young voters.

I'm certainly not comparing myself to Martin Luther King, Jr. or Mandela; I'm simply making the point that all master leaders have commonalities.

Mastery of leadership is not something you know or a place you eventually arrive at to rest on your laurels. Master leaders are people who practice the discipline, work at it, refine it, and live it day in and day out.

Master leaders—no matter their age, education, occupation, or the size of their bank accounts—are vision-driven, positive, exceptional human beings who live with integrity and make decisions that benefit themselves, others, and ultimately the world. Master leaders are distinctions in the cultural drift of mediocrity that we all navigate from birth to death.

We live in a world that shrugs its shoulders when our kids are gunned down in school. A world that thinks it's okay that our politicians behave more as "bullies-in-chief" than leaders—a world that lives in abject fear of standing up for change, for truth, for peace, for harmony, for love.

After more than 30 years as a transformational trainer, entrepreneur, and coach committed to creating leaders, I know this for sure: the world is crying—no, the world is screaming—for master leaders to take a stand, to change the status quo.

My vision is that this book will begin to respond to that cry.

What is the value of a master leader? Master leaders change the world. Imagine how master leaders wake up in the morning, how they operate in their lives. They wake with vision and operate as the cause of it, standing as the source of transformation for themselves and the world.

The world needs more master leaders. Your business needs them. Your family needs them. Your kids' schools need them.

You can become a master leader. How do I know? Because I've facilitated and fostered leadership in thousands of human beings. Because I'm an expert in personal and organizational transformation. I'm a master at coaching and understanding the psychology of leadership and human behavior. Because I've designed and facilitated thousands of transformational workshops in the United States, South America, and Europe for more than 30 years.

For all of that, you've likely never heard of me. I see myself as an ordinary person. I'm a husband in love with his wife. I'm an involved and active dad to five kids.

I'm passionate about golf and the Red Sox. I don't have a publicist and a huge brand. I'm not interested in becoming a trending topic on Twitter. My passions are my family and facilitating leadership in others.

My personal vision is to create peace, love, unity, and abundance for every man, woman, and child throughout the world. To achieve that vision, I must enroll other leaders in becoming master leaders. The more people and organizations who commit to mastering leadership, the closer my vision comes to reality. That's a win/win for all of us.

It's time for each of us to play the game of life at the highest level possible. When you picked up this book, you stepped into the game and have now taken the first step toward creating your own vision and mastery of leadership.

Congratulations! You've committed to cause the change you want to see in the world. Let's do it together. Lead on!

With Love,
Michael Strasner
Dallas, Texas
July 5, 2018

INTRODUCTION

THE CONTEXT OF TRANSFORMATIONAL LEADERSHIP

Leader: a person or thing that leads
Master Leader's definition: a person who makes a declaration to cause or create something unprecedented and then takes committed action to make it happen

Transformation: an act, process, or instance of transforming or being transformed
Master Leader's definition: a shift in our individual and collective beliefs that awakens new possibilities; the never-ending unfolding of possibility

I believe it's time for each of us to play the game of life this way: "All in, to win!" This book will give you specific tools and ways of being that you can learn and embody, tools that you can use to cause and create the future that you envision for yourself, your family, your community, your business, and ultimately, the world.

I believe that you—yes, you! —can master leadership, shift The Drift, and change the world.

Are you thinking, "Ok, Michael, I've read tons of leadership books, and I've heard all this before. How is this different?" Or, "I hope so, Michael. I've been trying to work up the courage to quit my job and start my business." Or is your conversation, "Can I really be a leader? Will people listen to what I have to say?" Or maybe, "I'll leave the responsibility of leadership to others. It's not my problem."

Whatever the internal conversation you're having with yourself—whatever stories you're telling yourself about your ability or inability to lead and impact change—I've heard it. And I'm saying you can change it.

Because here's the caveat that makes this book unlike other leadership books. Everything in it—every concept, every example, every leader presented—is filtered and delivered through the context of transformational leadership at the experiential level.

Leaders like Martin Luther King, Jr. and Harriet Tubman and Abraham Lincoln aren't remembered just because they were visionary (they were). Or inspiring (they were). We remember them because they fundamentally transformed us, the collective us. They lived their visions, experienced what they were creating in the moment, and by doing so asked us to turn our gazes to alternative perspectives, enrolled us in their visions for change, and awakened us to possibilities that didn't exist until they showed them to us.

By embodying their visions and modeling them for the world through their ways of being, they transformed our lives and the future by leading us to adopt their visions and make their visions our own.

Transformational leaders cause a shift in our individual and collective beliefs that awakens us to new possibilities; they show us a transformed world through a vision that is truly a win/win for everyone.

THE EVOLUTION OF TRANSFORMATIONAL LEADERSHIP

In January of 2018, I read an article in The New York Times titled, "Yale's Most Popular Class Ever: Happiness." The curriculum uses some of the same basic transformational techniques I've delivered in my training courses over the last three decades. The class is experiential, requires students to hold

2

themselves accountable, and focuses on assignments that result in behavioral change.

The "Happiness" class became so popular that an expanded version of the class is now available for free on Coursera as part of a seminar-style series on "the science of well-being." It is taught by original Yale course instructor Professor Laurie Santos.

If you had told me thirty, or twenty, or even ten years ago that Yale's curriculum included a class about happiness, I would have said: "You're out of your mind, there's no way. It's not possible." Because thirty years ago, experiential distinctions, coursework, and transformational language were seen as far outside of our collective comfort zones.

Back then, if you said something like, "master the possibilities" nobody knew what you were talking about. In general, people would shrug it off as some kind of "new age" thinking. Today, transformational language is so common that advertisers use it to sell us everything from technology to perfume to cars to golf clubs.

Thirty years ago, the idea of personal transformation or life coaching didn't exist as a career or profession. Now both are common. Transformational training centers such as Ascension Leadership Academy (ALA) in San Diego, Mastery in Transformational Training (MITT) in Los Angeles, Next Level Trainings in Columbus, Ohio, Espacio Vital Global (EVG) in Phoenix and El Paso, Impacto Vital in Mexico and Puerto Rico and Energia Positiva in Netherlands and Spain are increasingly popular and affordable. Transformational training happens globally.

In fact, Georgetown University's Institute for Transformational Leadership offers programs, workshops and training to "leaders and coaches dedicated to awakening, engaging, and supporting the leadership required in today's world to create a more sustainable and compassionate future" and "thought leadership on what it means to lead and coach in the context of the 21st century."

In 1978, historian and political scientist James M. Burns introduced the concept of transformational leadership in his book, *Leadership*, which won the Pulitzer Prize and the National Book Award and is still considered by many to be the seminal work in the study of modern leadership. In it, he examined the leadership styles of leaders throughout history—including those who misused their power—and debated and compared two types of leadership: transactional and transformational.

In 1999, Bernard M. Bass, Center for Leadership Studies, State University of New York, Binghamton, USA, compared transactional and transformational leadership this way: "The transformational leader emphasizes what you can do for your country; the transactional leader, on what your country can do for you."

Burns described transformational leaders as those who "have goals that transcend their own self-interests and work toward the common good of the followers." Bass built upon his definition. "Research evidence from around the world suggests that transformational leadership typically provides a positive augmentation in leader performance beyond the effects of transactional leadership. Furthermore, transformational leadership should be a more effective form of leadership globally because the transformational leader is consistent with people's prototypes of an ideal leader."

IN SEARCH OF CRITICAL MASS

Despite forty years of evidence that transformational leadership can transcend our currently practiced models of leadership—which clearly aren't working—we have not yet begun to reach critical mass.

Critical mass is a theory that states when a certain percentage of a group, or a population, or a culture (research is mixed between five percent and 25 percent as the tipping point) are enrolled, aligned and committed to the same thought, idea or vision, a rippling effect will occur. At the tipping point, the culture shifts.

My vision is to create like-minded leaders, people who are committed to transforming the culture and environment we live in, and who are committed to taking on the work of transformation and making it a way of life, a way of being.

Available at the tipping point of mastering leadership is critical mass that creates transformation. It can happen in a business, a family, a community. It occurs when enough people are enrolled in the vision, the message and the idea. And then the dominoes begin to fall, the ripples flow out, and transformation occurs.

But because transformation does not yet have a life of its own, it won't happen without intervention. It's not going to happen without someone standing up, using their voice, and having the courage to speak up and to stand for what's possible. The world doesn't transform, and won't transform, because we privately or secretly hope for peace or change or equality, or because we hope for joy and safety, or a great future for our children.

Transformation begins because one person stands up for change. And that person enrolls someone else to stand up, and that person enrolls someone else to stand up, and so on and so on until we create a critical mass that transforms the culture and the world we live in.

That someone is you! Imagine the possibilities you can create!

THE JOURNEY TO MASTER LEADERSHIP

The journey of transformation is the never-ending unfolding of possibility. And transformation is my life-long work.

In this book, I'll introduce you to and take you through a deep-dive excursion into the 12 Distinctions of Master Leaders. They're more than concept and theory. The distinctions are sharply-honed tools that are effective and powerful because they're time-tested and proven true, shaped from decades of experience. I know they work because I've coached and caused the visions and breakthroughs hundreds of thousands of students in transformational trainings and with coaching clients around the world.

You'll meet some of those students and clients in these pages; they are now master leaders who live the distinctions in their daily lives, professionally and personally.

I will also introduce you to the concept of The Drift, the automatic pilot of cultural norms all of us accept as reality. The Drift—in part because we're not aware of it—holds us back, keeps us chained and shackled to limiting beliefs and non-truths, and makes us believe that we are powerless in it.

This book is for you if you're someone who self-identifies as a leader even if you don't yet have the evidence and results to back up that leadership. You're a leader because you say so and act to move toward your dreams. This book is for you if others identify you as influential in some recognizable way; if you're one of those people who makes change happen at work, or in your family; or if you're a mover and a shaker, an innovator, a rainmaker, an entrepreneur.

Mastering Leadership is particularly valuable for politicians and community leaders, and those running large companies, including non-profits. The 12 Distinctions of Master Leaders are key knowledge for anyone who is in the work of making public policy and is inspired to make a deeper difference in the world, committed to producing greater results, and invested in contributing to society in meaningful ways.

If you've studied and taken on the work of increasing your own emotional intelligence (EQ), you'll be interested to know that recent research shows that transformational leaders rely on emotional intelligence more than transactional leaders. Using EQ, transformational leaders raise their level of consciousness and awareness about themselves, their relationship with the world around them, and the ways they show up in relationship to other people.

When master leaders combine the highest version of conscious self with the context and distinctions of transformational leadership, they create the potential to operate at a mastery level of leadership.

Wherever you are now in your leadership journey—whether you're young or old, an entrepreneur with a start-up, or a business leader with an established business, this book can be a springboard that supports and guides you to places you've never gone before. You can increase your ability to bring out a level of unity, passion, and inspiration in the people around you that was unthinkable in the past.

Because you're reading this book, I assume that you are, at the very least, committed to stretching into your own leadership, mastering communication, and elevating your results. Or that you've already reached a certain level of effectiveness as a leader, and now want to master your craft. In any case, it is your desire to sharpen your saw and use your life for a visionary purpose.

This book presents the opportunity and clarifies the responsibility for leaders like you—no matter your social, economic, or physical circumstances—to stand up and lead. To be an interruption in the status quo. To Shift The Drift and Change the World.

SHIFT THE DRIFT

Drift: a driving movement or force; impulse; impetus; pressure
Master Leader's definition: A cultural phenomenon since the beginning of human existence; a generational phenomenon passed on through communication, family teachings, traditions, education, and cultural norms. An invisible context of mediocrity; our societal status quo, our silently-agreed-upon accumulation of limiting beliefs, our collective autopilot.

Welcome, friends and fellow leaders, to The Drift. You're in it right now. It's all around you, all around us. We're wading in it, schlepping through it. The Drift continually laps at our ankles. We're born in it, we live in it, and we die in it. The Drift is global, though it looks one way in San Diego, another way in Boston, and yet a different way in Puerto Rico, or China, or Paris.

The Drift is an invisible context of mediocrity. It's our societal status quo, our silently-agreed-upon accumulation of limiting beliefs, our collective autopilot. It is a thick pea soup of unconscious apathy. It's where the stereotypes and assumptions live. It tastes like lethargy and it looks like distrust, like disconnection. It is where dreams and visions suffer and, ultimately, die.

THE DRIFT IS TIMELESS, AND IT LIES

The Drift is not new; it's perpetual. It changes as the beliefs of society morph and reflects the fictional norms a culture lives by at the time.

Let's take Galileo as an example of the timeless nature of The Drift. One day (around 1610) Galileo looked into his telescope and confirmed Copernicus's theory that the earth revolves around the sun rather than vice-versa, which went against the teachings of the Catholic Church. In 1616, the Church ordered Galileo to cease teaching this heresy. He didn't and went on to theorize and publicize that the rise and fall of the tides proved the movement of the earth. Outraged, the Church locked him up and kept him under house arrest until his death in 1642.

More than 350 years later, in 1992, Pope John Paul II officially declared that Galileo's theory was correct! Galileo's persecution and imprisonment were a result of the fictional belief systems of The Drift in the 1600s. It's interesting that the Church was so committed to being right that it took 350 years for them to own up to their part in it. Unfortunately, that didn't help Galileo!

When I was a kid, we learned that Christopher Columbus discovered America. We know now that many other explorers arrived before Columbus, not to mention the indigenous people who already occupied the land before them. Columbus opened the door to European colonization of North America that eventually led from his mission financed by the church of Spain to the Jamestown settlement financed by the church of England.

I contend that we (in U.S. society) are encultured in a belief system that completely discounts and ignores the fact that an entire race of indigenous Native Americans existed before us. In The Drift, our Judeo-Christian society view is that nothing exists until we say it exists. And when we say it exists, almost magically, it exists. This view allows us to say, collectively: we discovered America, and this land is ours because we discovered it, so whoever these people are that are on our land need to get off our land. And if they don't get off our land, we will push them off our land, no matter what it takes. We're still saying it. It's the immigration conversation in The Drift.

Current examples of the lies The Drift is telling us include: racism is over; global warming is a myth; "there are some good people," marching with white nationalist groups (as happened in the 2018 "Unite the Right" rally in Charlottesville, Virginia).

We're still teaching our kids that girls should act one way and boys another. That women who sleep around are easy and slutty but men who do it are cool and players. A woman who dominates in business is a bitch or acting like a man. But when a man dominates, he's considered a successful leader. The Drift perpetuates lies and double standards.

When The Drift speaks to us, it says, "Whatever you do, don't rock the boat. Even if you don't agree with the status quo, don't speak up. Don't call attention to yourself."

The Drift is often arrogant and talks this way: "He with the most toys wins." "I'm better than you." "I know." "I'm right." "I'm the best." "It's a dog-eat-dog world, and I'm a stable genius."

The Drift is invisible, but you can see it if you look for it. Give it a try. Glance up from your phone or desk for a minute. What do you see? I'm betting you see other people looking down at a screen, at the floor, at their coffee, at something other than you.

Stop and be present the next time you're in a crowd. Or on an elevator. Notice how no one makes eye contact and everyone — earbuds firmly in place — is staring past you, looking somewhere else, or following the floor numbers.

You'll see The Drift when you begin to observe what's going on around you. The next time you're on the road, watch commuters in traffic.

Better yet, go to your downtown area or wherever people in your world head off to work in the morning. Watch them. The going-to-work zombie apocalypse is its own Drift, and you can watch it moving in a Monday-Friday wave, trudging along, no connection, no authenticity, no substance, not rocking the boat. The Drift is numb and unaffected.

This is the world we live in. This auto-pilot we operate in is domesticated and encultured and ingrained in us. And it's constant. It's a thick muddy river. It's a human current that is here before us, exists while we're here, and will be here after we're gone.

The Drift is eternal and deep, with a relentless current that knocks many of us down.

BORN IN THE DRIFT

The Drift begins the same way for each of us.

Imagine yourself as a baby. When you were born, you were a blank canvas. And for the first few years of your life, you were completely free to be yourself. You laughed, you cried. You trusted everybody. You loved unconditionally. You didn't care how you looked and had no thoughts about doing it right or getting it wrong. You weren't cautious. You were a fully expressed, authentic little individual.

Seriously, think about it. Who needs coffee to wake up in the morning? Three-year-old you or adult you? Who cares about the size of their penis or their breasts? Three-year-old you or adult you? (Honestly, the 15-year-old you!) Who cares about whether they have a Buddha belly? Three-year-old you or adult you?

My point is that a three-year-old is authentic. A three-year-old doesn't live in the past; a three-year-old lives in the present. A three-year-old is creating and causing a life worth living moment to moment to moment.

What is a three-year-old into? Whatever they're into! They're all in! They open the box their new toy came in, and they climb into the box! They're literally in the box! Sometimes they don't even care about the toy.

They're immersed and engulfed in the experience, in the moment of doing whatever they're doing, and they're in joy and bliss. Look at a three-year-old who's happy and free all day, and then sleeps like a baby. Do you even remember the last time you slept like a baby (not including the times you drank too much)?

Our three-year-old selves, while born in The Drift, splash happily in it because they are unaffected by it. They aren't yet domesticated into their limiting belief systems. Sadly, those Drift-based belief systems eventually will shut down the unconditional full expression of their authentic selves.

DOMESTICATED IN THE DRIFT

Your domestication in The Drift began in childhood. Your adults invited three-year-old you to climb out of the literal box you were busy playing in and began to help you build an invisible box—one you would be stuck in for life—around your fully-expressed, authentic little self. That invisible box is now your comfort zone.

You built it piece by piece, experience by experience, along with your mom and dad, your grandparents, your older siblings, your teachers, your church, your friends, society, advertising.

They meant well, of course. They were teaching you the belief system of your culture and locale, and among those many lessons is the universal message of The Drift: "Keep it down. Put a lid on it. Look good. Fit in. Follow the rules because I said so. Stop. Little boys aren't supposed to do that. Little ladies are supposed to behave this way. Right. Wrong. Good. Bad. Be careful. No. You don't listen. Don't do that, what would people say? You can't. It's not possible. Why can't you be more like your sister? Turn it down. Shhh!"

These well-meaning lessons exist under the guise of "teaching" you how to be the best human being you can be, or to stop you from repeating someone else's mistakes, or to protect you from being hurt. Or maybe even—though it's counter-intuitive—to teach you how to be happy!

COMFORTABLE IN THE DRIFT

As we grow through childhood and adolescence, this control, feedback, and constant instruction/direction creates our comfort zones. The illusion of a comfort zone is that it is somehow warm and fuzzy, that it's a safe place to be.

This illusion is absolutely not true. Our comfort zone is a collection of self-limiting interpretations and beliefs that hold us back from creating our vision, dreams, and a life worth living. In the truest sense, our comfort zones protect and isolate us from authenticity and happiness rather than creating it.

We formulate our comfort zones through the following process: an event occurs, we experience feelings and emotion, we interpret, and then create a belief from those interpretations. As a result, we create a filtering system that we use as a lens to see and judge our lives. And we loop it continuously.

Here's a fundamental example:

Event: You're five years old. You fell off the swing in front of people, and they laughed at you.
Experience: pain and hurt.
Interpretation: embarrassment; fear of being hurt again.
Belief: You don't like heights; be cautious, be timid.

Another:

Event: You raise your hand in school to answer a question, and your friends start giving you dirty looks as if they're saying, "What are you doing raising your hand? You're a loser! Only losers raise their hand." And you put your hand down.

Experience: Embarrassment, shame, insecurity.

Interpretation: Shame, singled-out, fear of not being cool or looking good.

Belief: Don't speak up. Don't call attention to yourself. You're not good enough. You're not worthy.

One more:

Event: You're ten years old. Your father hits you because you didn't do your homework.

Experience: pain, sadness, anger, fear.

Interpretation: You're mad at your dad, or you don't like your dad, or you believe your dad is mean.

Belief: Your dad doesn't love you. You can't trust your dad. You should walk on eggshells. You are wrong, dumb.

Creating our comfort zones is a continual process: event, experience, interpretation, belief.

When we're very young, we don't necessarily create rock-solid beliefs and hold on to them until they're reinforced. But as we get older and our interpretations and experiences repeat, our beliefs get stronger.

Think of it this way: If your father spanks you one time when you're four, you're most likely not going to create a belief from it. But if your father is still hitting you when you're 15, you're definitely going to create a belief. And that belief will be something like, "I'm a piece of crap. He's an asshole, and he doesn't love me. I can't trust anyone. I need to get out of here as soon as possible."

The issues that keep you embedded in your comfort zone started when you were a child. Your beliefs about what you think about men, about women, about yourself, about the world, and about your place in the world were all established by the time you reached adolescence. And then you reinforced them with your choices, behaviors, and actions.

I'm a prime example. When I was 17 years old, I was rebellious. I didn't like myself. I didn't love myself. I was a good actor pretending to be cool, so I had a lot of friends. But at home, I thought I was totally worthless and didn't belong.

My parents said, "Michael, you should go to the University of Massachusetts (we lived in Boston). It's a great school and you're going to love it. A lot of your friends are going there. You're close to home. We could come and visit."

I heard that like nails on the chalkboard. My parents could come and visit? They won't come because they don't care about me! I'm not going to UMass. When I leave here, I'm not coming back. I'm getting as far away from here as possible.

So, I decided to go to Georgia Southern University. My parents said, "Michael, you shouldn't go to school in Georgia, and you won't like it. You won't fit in. It's still like the 1800's there, very backward and racist."

Of course, I said, "Okay, sign me up! I'm ready to go right now!"

At the time, I couldn't do ANYTHING that was in my own best interest. My own Drift inside The Drift was to sabotage myself at every opportunity. I didn't discover my unworthiness at Georgia Southern University. My unworthiness led me there.

Our beliefs are not created when we are 20- or 25-years old. They're built on a foundation we created as children. And unless we go through a transformational and interruptive process, most of us reinforce those beliefs for the rest of our lives.

Each time we reinforce a belief, the comfort zone gets a stronger wall because the walls of our comfort zone are constructed from our limiting beliefs and interpretations. Eventually that authentic, joyful three-year-old gets walled off, shut off, and shut down.

Ultimately, each of us lives in our comfort zone, treading water and controlled by The Drift. We're operating from certain behaviors and certain ways of being simply because that's what we were indoctrinated in and trained to believe.

THE DRIFT'S MANY FACES

What does your Drift look like? Have you spotted it yet?

I facilitate trainings, workshops, and seminars all over the United States and in various countries around the world. In all places, The Drift takes on the characteristics of geography and culture.

I grew up in Boston. In Boston, The Drift is often skeptical, appropriate and controlled. Boston is also parochial and territorial. Many people there live in comfort zones made of strong beliefs created by walking on eggshells and looking over their shoulders.

Traditionally and typically, Bostonians experience a sense of insecurity, inferiority, and fear of not being good enough. I fit right in! Bostonian insecurity may in part come from the city's constant competition with New York. You've likely heard some of New York's famous nicknames: The Big Apple, The City That Never Sleeps, King of the Hill, A-Number One (thank you, Frank Sinatra).

Bostonians live in the shadow of New York, and the constant comparison with it shows up in The Drift there.

When I was growing up, there was a certain side of the tracks, and, if you weren't from that side, or go to the right school, or come from the right town, The Drift might call you "less-than," segregate you, belittle you, look down upon you, and delegitimize you.

Over the years, Boston's immigrant population has grown, and those cultures have added their nuance—their norms, their nomenclature, their diversity—to The Drift. I went to high school in Brookline, a town founded by several wealthy and upper-class families who wanted to distance themselves from the poor Irish immigrants. Although Brookline is surrounded on three sides by Boston, the town is segregated by wealth, by haves and have-nots.

It's the same and also different in New York. New Yorkers tend to be extroverted, louder, more willing to say what they think; some might even say they're obnoxious. New Yorkers are more likely to live from aggressive, self-righteous, defensive comfort zones where they are always in a rush to get somewhere fast and get results at any cost.

The Midwest comfort zone is super nice. It's fine and peachy keen. It's somewhat submissive. In the south, it's stoic and polite. In California, it varies significantly, even from city to city. In San Diego, the comfort zone is casual; chill, slow, relaxed. Los Angeles, much like New York, is very aggressive, but its comfort zone is more about being cool and hip, being showy, having the best of everything, going to the best restaurants.

My point is this: The Drift is everywhere and, no matter the flavor or personality of the comfort zones created there, it expects something from you.

It expects you to be a certain way, behave the way everybody else behaves, wear the latest and the best. Fit in. Have an attitude. Hate the Yankees. Be conservative. Be liberal. Be right. Crush the competition. Shhh. Don't rock the boat. Pretend you're ok. Don't talk about politics, sex, or religion. Blame the government. Children are to be seen and not heard. If you have nothing nice to say, don't say anything at all. Lie. Fake news.

SURVIVAL IN THE DRIFT

Because we don't all fit in, can't possibly all behave, and simply do not meet the collective expectations of The Drift, it creates isolation, separation, insecurity, fear and resignation. We believe we don't count. Our votes don't count. Our voices don't count. We judge and criticize ourselves and each other, creating a conversation in The Drift that looking good and being right are more important than doing what works and feels authentic.

The Drift is exhausting. It's a full-time job to maintain our image, to worry about what people think of us all day long, to withhold communication, to walk on eggshells and tip-toe around not hurting anyone's feelings, not saying what we truly mean, not being honest in our relationships. Never asking for what we want. Having unrealistic expectations of our co-workers, employees, children, and life partners.

So instead, we hold back, don't risk, don't express ourselves genuinely. We're constantly worried about who we can trust, who cares about us. Does anyone really care? Can I do it? Do I matter? Can I make a difference?

Many of us are in shallow and superficial relationships because we're unwilling to be vulnerable and real. We have stress and pressure in our lives because we believe we're the Lone Ranger, without Tonto. We walk through life as victims, holding on to victim conversations from our past, believing everyone is out to get us, to hurt us, to let us down.

Comfortably numb has become the new normal for many people. We stay in relationships where the love is dead and gone, for convenience, to look good, for the children, or simply because it's better than being alone.

Many people have an arrogant chip on their shoulder and continually need to prove something, to make the doubters and haters wrong. They're always pushing, fighting, arguing, defending, protecting, in a narcissistic pursuit of filling up the coffers of emptiness they feel. Many of us use other people to satisfy our own needs, even for a few moments, to make us forget about the constant struggle to simply be enough.

The Drift is survival—our collective survival context of mediocrity.

FIGHT OR FOLLOW

Not all of us are content to just play along with this paradigm, of course.

Some people fight and resist The Drift, and some give up and give in. I find that most of the time people fall into one of two categories; they become rebels or followers.

Rebels resist control, resist people telling them what to do, what to think, how to act, how to behave. They're fighting the system. Fighting the box, fighting the comfort zone, fighting the culture. They're exhausted by fighting the environment and feeling as if they don't belong; they don't fit in. This resistance creates anger, frustration, isolation, separation, and insecurity. And fear, of course.

Followers often tell themselves they're fighting it, but they're playing along at happy hour. Or in the Monday-Friday zombie apocalypse workforce. And on their phones in between. Followers will do it all themselves and pretend to be happy.

Followers take what they can get. The crumbs; the end of the loaf. They think everything is their fault, that they're not good enough, or unlucky, or an accident. They don't speak up or use their voice when it matters. Their silence often makes the unacceptable okay. This creates deep feelings of powerlessness, sadness, depression, invisibility, insignificance, and resignation.

Where's the joy in that? There's no inherent happiness in The Drift. There's no purpose in it. There's no vision in it. The Drift can't create a life worth living. It's survival.

Why would anyone want survival when a life worth living—a life of freedom, power, confidence, love, inspiration, passion, and contribution to the world—is possible?

TRANSFORMATION IN THE DRIFT

One of the things I've learned while engaged in transformational leadership over the last 30 years is that change happens in the world in one of four ways: revolution, evolution, extinction or transformation.

When I look at those forms of change, only one is a win/win possibility for all. And it's transformation.

Transformation doesn't have a life of its own because it's not normal. What's normal is to "shut up." What's normal is to "keep it down." What's normal is to be a drifter in The Drift, to be someone who sucks the tailpipe of mediocrity. What's normal is not to request a raise from your boss because you deserve it. What's normal is "do as I say, not as I do." What's normal is passive-aggressive behavior. What's normal is to play small. What's normal is to be selfish. What's normal is to stay in a relationship while making excuses for its breakdowns and conditions. What's normal is to try to get away with things, to manipulate. What's normal is to lie, and then lie on top of a lie, to cover up the lie. What's normal is men and women cheat. What's normal is people make babies, but they don't raise those babies into healthy, responsible, contributing citizens who realize the gifts they have and share them with the world.

Transformation won't happen on its own because transformation is not in the context of the culture and society we live in. Transformation in The Drift means moving people from the survival context of status quo and comfort zone into a whole new paradigm, a whole new way of being and living life.

The idea of transformation asserts that people can evolve into a higher level of consciousness; they can break through the walls of their comfort zones and return to their authentic selves. They can lead, have a voice, have a vote (and use it), be loving with their families, be responsible in raising their children. People can be in magical partnership with their spouses or life partners and learn to compromise, be of high integrity, be genuine, live by and honor their word, and create a deep and profound love and respect for one another.

TAKING A STAND IN THE DRIFT

The idea of transformational leadership is that you stand up in The Drift when you create a vision for what's possible for all. It's a win/win vision. Master leaders shamelessly interrupt the automatic pilot of the cultural norms that the world accepts. Interrupting The Drift by standing for transformation expands transformation, makes it a real possibility, and brings life to the living.

When a leader becomes a distinction in The Drift they rise up and force the current of The Drift to go around them. Martin Luther King, Jr. (MLK) comes to my mind when I think about transformational leaders. MLK shifted The Drift.

He stood up when people told him to sit down and shut up. People said, "It's not your place." He said thank you for sharing and stood up anyway. The world wanted to keep him down. He rose up. He didn't rise up as an ego-driven, angry rebel like I was as a kid. He rose up as a courageous leader. He rose up as a visionary. He rose up and reminded us of our beginnings, that, "We hold these truths to be self-evident that all men are created equal."

And he defied the cultural drift of maintaining the status quo. During MLK's time, it's likely most African American people felt that they were not only victims to their situation or circumstance, but also felt a sense of resignation, a deep feeling of fatalism to the racism itself. Of course, in our societal Drift, we have also created a powerful, centuries-old environment of institutional racism, from voting, to career, to economics, to education, and so on. But MLK wasn't enrolled in that societal environment. Through education, eloquence and his powerful message, he demonstrated and showed all of us what's possible when we own our voices and vote.

The Drift often resists and nips at the heels of those who take a stand in it. In 2018, Fox News host Laura Ingraham told NBA star LeBron James to "Shut up and dribble," after he voiced an opinion about politics and racism regarding Donald Trump.

Several months later, James opened the "I Promise" School for at-risk children in his hometown of Akron, Ohio. The school is a partnership between Akron and the LeBron James Family Foundation. He also is producing a three-part documentary series for Showtime chronicling the history of the NBA and the influence of its players on social issues, politics, and pop culture. The title? "Shut Up and Dribble."

As I've said previously, transforming The Drift is not going to happen without intervention. It's not going to happen without people—master leaders—who use their voices and have the courage to speak up and to stand for what's possible.

Transformation will happen because somebody like you will stand up and enroll someone else to stand up, and that person is going to enroll someone else to stand up and so on until we create a critical mass to transform the culture and the world that we live in.

Of course, a win/win for the world means a win/win for you too. When you transform yourself, you release that three-year-old you boxed in long ago. What does that mean? What does that look like? Your authentic expresses itself naturally and without limits.

When you're happy, you express your full happiness. You don't tamp it down because your mother or your classmates or co-workers tell you to keep it down, to not draw attention to yourself.

When you're happy, you fully self-express. You let it rip. When you're feeling confident about something, you own your voice, and you speak up in a committed, intentional, confident way.

And equally, when you're sad, you express your sadness. You don't hold it back because you're worried about what someone else thinks or fake it because you don't want to let go of control.

Lisa Kalmin is principal and founder of WorldWorks Trainings and co-founder of Inspire Coaching. She sees the opportunities available in shifting The Drift.

"The Drift represents the human conspiracy, the unconscious human conspiracy. We're born into it, but we don't know we're in it; it's like we're fish in water. If a fish never knows it's in water, then it has no way to distinguish another possibility. When people can see what's truly possible and stand up in The Drift it means they take a stand for their own power and responsibility; they become generators of their own life. They don't have to default to what the "drift" says they should be or do. Other people see them standing and want to stand as well."

SHIFT THE DRIFT AND CHANGE THE WORLD

In the following chapters, I'm going to introduce you to the 12 Distinctions of Master Leaders, a tool I use to train leaders in transformation all over the world.

These are distinctions and ways of being that are valuable for everybody and anybody, but they're not going to happen automatically. Transformation is rising above The Drift to create a distinction, a life worth living, a life of authenticity, a stand for something bigger then self-preservation.

Authenticity doesn't take work. Authenticity is complete unbridled and unhindered freedom, the freedom to choose the life you want to live and the difference you are committed to making. Transformation is stepping into and up to your greatness, shedding the masks and barriers that shackle you from your creativity and ultimate gifts. It's the rediscovering of your authentic self.

"We forget how joyful life can be when we're in The Drift. So, we need extra help to be fun—alcohol and cigarettes and marijuana. We need the party to stimulate ourselves," says my friend and transformational trainer Ricardo Tirado of the Dominican Republic. "But when you're working on yourself and your vision for the world you get high on your own stuff. And when you can do that, you have to stand up in The Drift."

The world is waiting for your joyful three-year-old.

**SHIFT THE DRIFT
AND CHANGE THE WORLD**

Connect with your tangible and intangible results. Look at your relationships What are the limiting patterns? Fears, judgments, insecurities?

_____

_____

_____

_____

_____

_____

_____

_____

_____

What are the conditions of The Drift where you live? How do you contribute to it?

_____

_____

_____

_____

_____

_____

_____

_____

What are the culturally expected thoughts and behaviors in your particular observance of The Drift? In your family? Community?

_____

_____

_____

_____

_____

_____

_____

_____

_____

_____

What opportunities exist for you to shift The Drift and change the world?

_____

_____

_____

_____

_____

_____

_____

_____

_____

_____

DISTINCTION 1

VISION: WHERE LEADERSHIP BEGINS

Vision: the act or power of anticipating that which will or may come to be.

Master Leader's definition: an operational context for life that overtakes the ego and becomes the fuel that drives actions; a declaration to create something in the future; the possibility to create an unprecedented life and living experience for self and the world.

"My vision for the world is to end the epidemic mindset of fundamental scarcity so people can see what's available for them when they choose to be abundant in every imaginable way. When we regularly invest in ourselves and also are generous with our energy (time, money, and talents) we ALL rise together." – Jenna Phillips Ballard, co-founder, Ascension Leadership Academy

---

Master leaders have a powerful vision. "Vision" is often considered synonymous with words such as "dream," "goal" or "mission." However, as it pertains to master leadership, the meaning of vision is distinctive. A visionary is someone who brings the future into the present. Visionaries are pioneers who stand in the future as if it has already occurred, not as they hope it will be someday.

Master leaders develop ideas that most never imagine; ideas that when created are a benefit to humankind in some way. Many people have flashes of an idea that may seem extraordinary in the moment, but what usually happens is the idea becomes a fantasy, a nice dream that might happen but probably won't.

Master leaders take an ordinary idea and turn it into a burning desire and vision that becomes irresistibly contagious to others. True leadership cannot exist without vision, and true vision is a compass for every aspect of life. For master leaders, vision is a context to operate from, and it creates something that cannot happen without their full participation.

A VISION-DRIVEN LIFE

I declared a personal vision 32 years ago. My vision is to create peace, love, unity, and abundance. Yet my vision is not just about me. My vision is a win/win for everyone, including you.

Vision is declaring the existence of something in the future that is unprecedented, unpredictable and does not yet exist. Vision is declaring that you're going to create something in the future that takes your quality of life and your experience of living and brings it into being, into a higher level of consciousness. Vision is not something that just happens. It's something you declare. Something you create.

For me, it looks like this: I wake up in the morning and begin consciously creating the future that I declared—an unprecedented future, a future that is unpredictable, that would not have happened without my full participation in it. And I do that daily, whether it's with my wife, my children, my co-workers, my business partners, or my community. My vision drives my life.

It is possible to create the life of your dreams and a win/win for the world. It's not a new concept. Author Thomas Moore introduced the concept of a Utopian life in the 14th century as "a place of ideal perfection especially in laws, government, and social conditions."

What are you thinking right now? Are you asking (maybe from your comfort zone in The Drift), "Really, Strasner? You want me to believe I can create Utopia?" Yes. Why not? We all create The Drift and have since the beginning of humankind.

Through vision, a Utopian life—an unprecedented life, for each of us and all of us—is possible. Even if we aren't likely to see it happen for all in our lifetimes, isn't it worth exploring and creating now?

VISION MAXIMIZES LIFE

When most people think of a concept like Utopia, they roll their eyes, which makes sense, of course. Most people live in The Drift, and such concepts can't survive there.

What survives in The Drift is playing small, minimizing, and cynicism.

Most people (not you...well, maybe you) are living a life that's good, fine, okay, with a lot of to-dos. A life full of obligations and "have-tos." I have to take my kids to school. I have to pick up the dry cleaning. I have to go to work. I have to pay my bills and taxes.

Most people live in a place of good/fine/okay. Their job's okay. Their kids are good. Their spouse is fine.

Just for fun and illustration, let's say our kids go to school together and I run into you on the street, and we have this conversation:

Me: Hi, John! Good to see you! How are you doing?
You: Okay, Michael. I'm fine.

Me: How's work?

You: It sucks right now, but I'm hanging in there. Gotta make the donuts, you know?

Me: How are your kids? I saw Nick at football practice yesterday when I was picking up Savannah from cheerleading. He's got a rocket for an arm!

You: Yeah, yeah. His mom's worried about him playing football, but what are you gonna do? Good to see you, Michael, gotta go pick up the dog from the vet."

Sound familiar? How often do you have this kind of conversation? Please note: if I run into you on the street, I will more than likely probe and ask questions to connect with you on a deeper level. To do so is in alignment with my vision.

This is a normal, everyday conversation. It's the way we live and communicate in our society. The point is, there's nothing wrong with a good/fine/okay life. But it's not a vision-driven life, and it's not a life that creates master leaders. This conversation occurs with minimal authenticity, depth or "real" connectivity. It's complete automatic pilot.

Automatic pilot shows up in minimizing those things we like, even those things we love. I talk to hundreds of people a week, and it's common for them to minimize what's happening in their lives, and particularly in their relationships. I might ask a male friend, "How's your relationship? How's your wife? And even if he's deeply in love with his wife, he'll say something like, "We're okay; she's fine." Or, "She's good."

Those are common answers in The Drift because it's not safe to say to your male friends, "Wow, I am so in love with my wife!" Why? We humans (especially men) are trained by The Drift to downplay our emotions and feelings, and our ability to express them. We've trapped them inside of our comfort zones, and we rarely invite them out to play.

For contrast, let's imagine that a conversation like this happens while I'm on the golf course:

Joe: Hey, Michael. How's your wife? How's Hillary?

Me (making direct eye contact with Joe): Hey Joe, thank you for asking! I want to tell you something. Hillary is the most beautiful woman that ever walked on the face of the earth. My wife is the most intelligent, generous, thoughtful, sexy, amazing human being I have ever met. I am literally pinching myself that I get to have this relationship! I am the luckiest man alive! Thank you for asking!

Can you imagine that conversation happening on the golf course? Or by the water cooler in the office? I'm one of only a few men I know that would answer the question that way. You know what men talk about on the golf course? They talk about sports, money, business, the stock market and yes, sometimes women. But they don't talk about their wives and how much they love them. Some of them don't even wear their wedding rings.

I never take my wedding ring off. I don't take my ring off because I'm in love with my wife. My ring is a constant symbol and reminder of my commitment, devotion, and fidelity. I don't minimize my relationship with my wife. I celebrate it and MAXIMIZE it because it's my vision to create an unprecedented, unimaginable life with her.

It is possible to bring alive a vision for your life, your relationships, and your future that doesn't include minimizing. You can bring alive a vision that maximizes and accentuates your experience, that brings out your highest form of being, your best version of yourself. Actually, that's the only way to create the magic that's possible and available in your personal relationships because emotions and feelings play a central role in the quality of the experience.

ENVISIONING YOUR UNIMAGINABLE LIFE

I create my vision for my unimaginable life (meaning beyond my wildest dreams) continually, and anyone can use this method.

I look into the future and view it without blinders, without limitation, without barbed wire, without filtering it through past interpretations and experiences. I look at my life and visualize how the future will be if it is exactly the way I want it to be for myself and the world around me. And then I use all of my tools to create it.

Most of us do a fabulous job of conjuring up the many obstacles that might get in the way of achieving our wildest dreams because that's what we learn in The Drift. The Drift says, "be careful, don't get too excited because there's another shoe waiting to drop, and by the way, the light at the end of the tunnel is a train."

Our minds are tools that invite us to dream of anything and everything; they're not just information-gathering devices that suck in data, analyze it, and spit it back out. Our minds are tools of creativity, and I use mine like a brush to paint my future. A future that is rich, deep, meaningful, purposeful; a future where I joyfully experience the full expression of who I am (you know, like a three-year-old!)

In my vision of my future, I have access to any and all the ways of being that are necessary to create the life I'm envisioning—a future that is unprecedented, unimaginable, and so profound that even seeing it at the highest level of imagination it's beyond my wildest dreams.

A visionary master leader is someone who brings the future into the present. Not once, not twice, but continually.

WHAT DO YOU WANT?

What do you want? For your family? For your business or career? For the world? What do you want the substance of your life to be about? What do you stand for?

Start with a blank slate, a blank canvas, a blank sheet of paper, and begin to articulate your life. You have unlimited ways to create and craft your vision and countless books and websites dedicated to the how-tos of doing so. If you'd like a future-creating tool, there are several leadership training centers on the resources page in the back of the book, and you can research tools and apps online. Find one that resonates with you.

Imagine yourself in the future—one, two, five, ten, twenty years out—both personally and professionally. What is the life of your dreams? You have no limitations here. Write it down and describe it in detail. Write it from the point of view that it's happening now, as if you are in the future, right now.

The point is to use your tools, your mind, and hands to begin to get your vision out of your head and ultimately in some physical form.

As you paint that picture and create your Utopian life, you must see it and experience it fully right down to the color of the plush rugs in your dream home, to the new-car smell of your black hardtop convertible BMW with Harman Kardon stereo. In your vision, you already know the touch of your future partner, have the career of your dreams, and determine your own abundant income.

Be sure to include the emotional experiences you want in the life of your dreams. What do you want? Is it love, connectivity, passion, intimacy, fun, adventure, freedom, joy, energy, fulfillment, satisfaction? Something else? It's your future. You choose. Do you have separate visions for your personal and professional lives? Get specific.

Master leaders are convinced that the reality of their creation will materialize in measurable results. To reach mastery, it is essential to continually recognize the power of creative imagery, to practice it, and to know without a doubt that you, and you alone, are the author of your future.

Know what you want. See your perfect Utopian life. Be in continuous creation of it and relationship with it.

CHOOSE YOUR WAYS OF BEING

Quite often, people think that creating a stunning vision board and meditating in front of it every day will bring the future into existence. It won't. One of my students wrote herself a check for one million dollars and stuck it on the ceiling over her bed, convinced that if she just concentrated on it hard enough before she went to sleep every night, the money would show up in her bank account within the year. It didn't.

True vision dives much deeper, down past the sparkly objects and fancy cars and dream jobs and perfect partners most of us focus on. Crafting a win/win, master-leader vision requires that you also imagine and manifest the ways of being that will lead you to create, sustain and live your vision, a vision that becomes the operational context for your life, that overtakes your ego and becomes the fuel that drives your actions.

A way of being is simply the way you choose to show up in the world. All of us can choose infinite ways of being—we have no limitations. You create and embody a way of being by tapping into your emotional self ("my wife is the most beautiful woman in the world; she glows from the inside out!" vs. "she's fine") and using it to bring into reality the experiences that you're committed to creating.

For example, you might choose to be loving, to show up in the world as love. You bring that way of being to life when you consistently behave and show up as vulnerable, connected, sensitive, generous, kind, compassionate, empathetic.

Visualize yourself as a powerful, courageous, confident, risk-taker in the pursuit of your business vision. Successful entrepreneurs embody a relentlessness sense of passion and are intoxicating with their ways of being.

In your future-painting, imagine exactly how you're showing up, how you're living, how you're being, and how you are participating in creating the world to make it exactly how you want it to be.

Your vision will include three to five guiding ways of being or relational principles that bind the vision together.

Early in this chapter, I gave you my vision involving peace, love, unity, and abundance. These ways of being influence every choice I make personally and professionally.

If I am committed to creating peace, I act and behave in ways that create peace. If I am committed to a vision that includes unity in the world, I act in ways that create unity in my own life. If my vision is to live in an abundant world, I must live an abundant life that is plentiful and rich in all ways—not just those that include dollar signs. If I want a world that is loving, I must be loving. These are the ways of being I filter my day-to-day and minute-to-minute choices through. They're interconnected, inter-related, and ongoing.

Throughout this book, you'll see examples of how my ways of being and the ways of being of other master leaders show up in and are transforming the world.

My friend and former student Mike Bacile owns a company in Texas called The Daily Java. The company's mission and tagline are: Building a Community One Cup at a Time by Enabling Others to Make a Difference in the World. Mike's personal vision? "I change the world."

Mike lives his vision in his business, of course. But his vision was inspired by family.

When Mike's daughter Angela was born in 2000, he wanted, as most parents do, to build a safer world for her. So Mike looked into the future and imagined Angela at age 18 with a flat tire on the side of the road and set out to increase the odds that whoever pulled up behind her on that road would help her rather than hurt her.

"That vision wakes me up and drives me," Mike said. "What that means in the big picture and how it touches me personally is I realize that I'm not going to be able to change everybody, but the more people I affect, the more difference it makes. I'm just trying to change the odds, to create better odds of people treating others with respect, valuing life. I want to change the way we communicate and deal with each other as human beings. My ultimate vision is that I want to change the world. But on a selfish level, it's about my children."

That's a master-leader vision.

Business leader Evan Hackel is the founder and principal of Ingage Consulting, a frequent keynote speaker, and the author of *Ingaging Leadership: 21 Steps to Elevate Your Business*. Evan's personal vision is "to help contribute to others and to make other people feel loved and accepted."

Evan believes in creating a shared vision and building it into the culture. "The common core of my vision for my businesses is to do unique things that help companies exceed at exponential rates so that they are—not marginally successful or highly successful—but exceptionally successful. I own several different businesses, and I invest in many others. Vision is a very important attribute of what I do."

VISION BENEFITS ALL

When I connect with my vision, everybody benefits. Period. There is no "except for" or "not those people" possible in my vision. Who wins in my vision? Everyone. Me. You. Vision values all. Vision benefits all.

Few of our leadership models are built on vision. Many of our current leaders are not acting from vision. Donald Trump's vision, "Make America Great Again," sounds like a vision. But it isn't. It's not transformational.

I am proud to be an American, and I stand for America and the ideals and principles it is founded upon. That said, I believe that the phrase "Make America Great Again," is a standard belief of The Drift. It assumes that America is not great, which is not leadership—it's a disempowering and divisive judgment. It's comparing something to the way it was before vs. focusing on the way it can be in the future, without precedent.

By the way, when in time was America great? When people had to hide their sexuality? When black people and women couldn't vote? When we were at war with Viet Nam? When women were expected to be homemakers? Or maybe before Barack Obama was president? Hmmm…it really makes me wonder at what time and what place American was "great," and what Trump is referring to that's missing in today's America.

Vision is not judgment. Vision is not comparison. Vision is not a reaction to something. Vision isn't making something wrong and declaring how bad it is now compared to what it used to be. Vision is not creating something that has happened before or recreating something (that's recycling).

It seems that Donald Trump wants to create a future that works only for himself, his family, and for the people who elected him to office. If he were a master leader, he would be communicating a clear vision and making choices that represent all Americans. Based on what I hear and see, his "vision" is not a vision for a future that works for all of us. Getting results at any and all costs is more a business strategy than a vision for the President of the United States.

True vision creates an empowering and uplifting future that works for everybody. I want to live in a world where people like Theo Epstein, Melinda Gates, Alex Cora, Serena Williams, Tim Cook, Oprah, and Bono are not anomalies.

I want to live in a world where standing up for and declaring your vision is the norm rather than the outlier. Where "that's just the way it is" means we're collectively living in a vision of a future we're excited to embrace.

As my friend, mentee and transformational trainer Felipe (Pipe) Avila says: "If you think you're a leader and you don't want a better world for everybody, you're not really a leader."

VISION:
WHERE LEADERSHIP BEGINS

What is your vision?

_____

_____

_____

_____

_____

_____

_____

_____

_____

What unprecedented and extraordinary future are you creating?

_____

_____

_____

_____

_____

_____

_____

_____

_____

What are the details of your unimaginable life? What experiences and relationships are included?

_____

_____

_____

_____

_____

_____

_____

_____

_____

_____

What ways of being will you use to bring the vision into reality?

_____

_____

_____

_____

_____

_____

_____

_____

_____

_____

DISTINCTION 2

COMMITMENT TO VISION: AUTHORSHIP AND CAUSE

Commitment: to pledge oneself to a position on an issue or question; express (one's intention, feeling, etc.).
Master Leader's definition: to give your word to be and do whatever it takes to cause the vision to become reality. To live as your word. To put yourself at stake for the vision.

"Commitment to my vision means the role I play doesn't matter because I'm going to lead no matter what."
– Mary Jo Lorei, transformational trainer and coach

Master leaders are committed to their vision. It is not enough to have a vision. To manifest a vision, leaders must be flexible in their approach. If a leader is truly committed to the vision, she/he must be willing to do whatever it takes and embody a powerful way of being that is unlike ordinary, normal ways of being. Master leaders understand that commitment is what transforms vision into reality.

Commitment speaks boldly of one's intention and actions that speak louder than words. Commitment is making time when there is none, coming through day after day and year after year. It is the power to change the face of anything with an unbridled passion for making it happen. A vision or a dream is a nice idea—a fantasy—unless there is commitment behind it.

Commitment is the bridge that connects the vision with the results. Remember that a vision creates something that wasn't going to happen anyway—an unprecedented, unpredictable, unimaginable life. Your vision is a declaration to cause something in the future that is inspiring, meaningful, deep, rich, purposeful and transformative; a future that brings out the best in who you are, in your authentic self.

When you are committed to your vision, you're sharing and living in it, creating the results that are consistent with the vision, creating the personal and professional life experiences that are consistent with the vision.

With commitment, your vision expands and ripples out from you to the world.

WITHOUT COMMITMENT VISION IS JUST A FANTASY

Vision without commitment is a nice idea. It's hyperbole. It's a fantasy.

Let's experiment with that thought. What if, metaphorically, you and I sit together, and we look into each other's eyes, hold each other's hands, light a candle, and play John Lennon's "Imagine." We connect with the beauty of the song, and we imagine a world that is full of peace, love, joy, freedom, and infinite possibility; all of the things that we imagine the world to be in our vision. And then we blow the candle out, hug each other, and say goodbye.

What's actually happened in that metaphorical scenario? Did we maybe have an experience of that vision? Yes. Did we have an experience of what might be possible through that vision? Yes.

But have we manifested the vision? Is the world transformed? Is our business transformed? Are our families transformed? Are our lives transformed? Are we now living our vision because we had this moment? The answer is no.

Let's expand on it, make the experiment bigger. What if we enlarge that one-on-one experience to a group and now ten or 20 or 50 or 100 of us are together, and we light a candle and play "Imagine" again? We close our eyes; we visualize the future, the world, and how all of us want it to be. What's happened then?

Nothing. Nothing's transformed. We probably shared an empowering or touching experience, but nothing tangible has occurred because we haven't taken any new actions.

What bridges the gap between vision (the idea of something) and the realization—the facts, the evidence, the results-altering, world-changing transformation of the vision—is commitment. And commitment shows up in actions.

COMMITMENT PUTS YOUR STAKE IN THE GROUND

What commitment means in the context of the vision is simply this: you put your word and yourself at stake for something.

When I say put yourself at stake, it means you're putting yourself on the line. You're declaring that you're giving your word to the vision, and when you say that you're giving your word to the vision, that you're at stake for it, it means you're vulnerable. You're vulnerable to success, and you're vulnerable to failure.

Michael Chiang is living such a declaration. Michael is the founder of Eleven Recruiting, a company committed to "staffing with a purpose." His vision is to give opportunities to children in low-income areas, change their beliefs about what they can achieve, graduate high school, and pursue a life through education.

Here's the at-stake piece of Michael's vision. He walked away from a lucrative career to start Eleven Recruiting and is giving 11 percent of his net earnings to nonprofit organizations that support community and education. I asked Michael to tell me about some of his significant achievements in that process. He said, "Having the courage to step away from the financial abundance I'd created for myself to start my own company, to become an entrepreneur. I left half a million dollars a year on the table to begin something, to launch my vision."

Master leaders like Michael are deeply committed to vision. He is authoring, causing, and even financing the change he wants to see in the world!

When you declare and genuinely commit to the vision, the vision calls you forth to create an unprecedented future, and unimaginable possibility, whatever that is for you, and you step into the actions that are consistent with the vision.

When you put yourself at stake, no other possibility exists except this: You're the author of the vision, the owner of the vision, the cause of the vision. It can't happen without you. Your vision begins to manifest through action, through your ways of being, through your words and actions. Commitment permeates the entirety of your life.

When you say you are committed to your vision, it means you give your word, and you step into the power of your word. When you give your word to achieve your vision, it means you declare that you will consistently and rigorously follow through with it in every choice you make, in every decision you make, in every aspect of your life.

MACRO INTO MICRO

The act of being the author and cause of your vision becoming a reality is also the act of bringing the macro into the micro. Causing your vision to manifest in the world means that you, as a master leader, take it from a general/non-specific, Utopian idea to behaviors and actions that show up in the moments of your life.

Let's say you have a vision to cause and create abundance in your job, and suppose you work in a sales job with quotas to fulfill and complete. Suppose the expectation is that you will sell 50 units by such and such a date, and you have a vision for abundance. Of course, you want to double that sale to 100 units.

To achieve that goal and live in the vision of abundance, you must act consistently in the ways of being of abundance. To determine the ways of abundance, imagine the ingredients that make up abundance. Who do you admire that is creating abundance in the world? How does that person show up in life in relationship to abundance? Confident, powerful, dynamic, courageous, risk-taking, inspiring?

Now see yourself in this visualization of abundance. How will you show up in your sales call? In the next sales presentation? Are you coming from abundance? Are you rich with your thoughts? Are you choosing based on plenty? Is your attitude generous? Is your energy abundant?

What makes a vision real and breathes life into it in actions, choices, behaviors and—ultimately—outcomes, is the connection to the macro vision in micro moment-to-moment behaviors. And of course, being fully committed to the vision.

Again, whether the vision for abundance is for a relationship, starting your dream company, or for the world in general, it becomes a reality in the daily details.

Ryan Clarkin is a mindset expert and transformational coach who works with entrepreneurs, coaches, and influencers to create the impact in life they desire. Ryan is gifted at bringing the macro in the micro.

His vision is "to create a world where everyone chases their dreams with relentless passion, a world where people believe that they can live a life of their own design, a world where people know that they matter, where school shootings are replaced with hug campaigns, bullying is replaced with empowerment, and judgment is replaced with love. His vision for people is that they truly know how powerful they are, believe in themselves, go after what they want, and live a full, fulfilling life that they will look back on in awe at the moment of its completion."

Ryan intentionally and consciously exemplifies daily commitment through his ways of being and actions, drilling down the big-picture version of his vision to the smaller day-to-day interactions with others.

"I'm true to myself in going after my own dreams and being the example. Being the example and making it normal to be and live at 100 percent has a powerful effect on the people around me," he said. "Whether I interact with a waiter at a restaurant, the person behind me in line, or just someone I cross paths with, I set an intention to make a difference with that person, to bring alive my vision of self-love and self-acceptance. I want to wake up a dream so deep within their heart that they become inspired to take action on it like their life depends on it, because the life of their dreams does."

AUTHOR AND CAUSE

To me, being the author and cause of my vision becoming a reality means I'm not settling for mediocrity. Complacency is unacceptable. I'm taking a stand in The Drift to say mediocrity is not okay.

Let's look at health as an example. If I am to author and cause my declared vision of peace, love, unity, and abundance, I must do it from a place of health. Whether I like it or not, whether I feel like it or not, I'm going to the gym. I'm going to work out. I'm going to eat well. I'm going to say no to alcohol and say yes to green vegetables (which doesn't mean I won't have a beer, glass of wine or a tequila shot every now and again).

In health and all other endeavors, my actions reflect my vision. I've given my word. And if I break my word, if I don't live my word, my vision has no power.

Losing the vision is losing the purpose. It's losing the fuel. Vision is the fuel that drives our actions.

Let's go back to the context of The Drift, this cultural phenomenon of which no one person is the author. The Drift is the collective compilation of the automatic pilot of human behavior and the cultural norms that come out of it.

The Drift—unless it's interrupted—essentially predetermines the outcome of our lives and our experiences of living. I'm in The Drift, you're in The Drift, we're all in The Drift, all the time. When you declare your vision and commit to it, you interrupt it and become a distinction in the river, in the flow, that is The Drift. You become an island, and now the current must move around you. It no longer carries you along. It no longer overwhelms you. You actually rise above it.

Without commitment, without vision, you're contributing to The Drift. I like to think of The Drift as a mighty river. You're the source of what happens to you in that river. Does it exist outside you? Yes, of course. Was it here before you? Yes, of course. Will it be here after you? Yes, of course.

Visionary master leaders who are committed to being the author and cause of their inspired lives, leaders who live by their word, can and do shift The Drift. They've ceased contributing to its fiction and unconsciousness. Instead, they are guiding through the values, principles, and behaviors of transformation and leadership.

**COMMITMENT TO VISION:
AUTHORSHIP AND CAUSE**

Now that you have a vision, what does it mean to be committed to it?

What committed actions will it take to achieve your vision?

DISTINCTION 2 – COMMITMENT TO VISION

What is real and authentic commitment? Do you pay prices for not living as your word?

_____

_____

_____

_____

_____

_____

_____

_____

_____

_____

_____

How can you use Distinction 2 to Shift the Drift?

_____

_____

_____

_____

_____

_____

_____

_____

_____

DISTINCTION 3

VALUES: CREDIBILITY THROUGH RIGOR

Values: the ideals, customs, institutions, etc., of a society toward which the people of the group have an affective regard.
Master Leader's definition: the principle-based pillars that hold up your vision.

> "Quite simply, mastery of leadership means constantly living in my vision even when I don't feel like it, even when I don't want to, even when it gets hard. Mastering leadership is living, eating, sleeping, and breathing it. No matter what." – Jennifer Sconyers, President and Founder,

Master leaders live by values that are consistent with their vision. For master leaders, values are the single most important foundational decision-making criteria. Look around you. It is easy to notice those "leaders" in our world who say all the right words but don't live up to what they are saying. They may have results that appear valuable to the world, but they don't have respect (at least not the kind of respect that inspires others to follow in their footsteps).

True leaders do not hide from asking and answering compelling questions. Their attitudes, decisions, behaviors, and actions are rigorously aligned and consistent with the visions they declare important. Most significantly, they are authentic and honest about their results.

Master leaders, committed to author and cause their visions, embody and embrace those values. They are in consistent action, creating and manifesting their visions, and are continually asked and tasked with choices and decisions that can move them toward, or away from, manifesting those visions. The values leaders choose to live by—with consistency and rigor—inform every one of those decisions.

The strategy to get there is to create a set of values to filter your choice-making and decision-making processes through as you act on your vision.

VALUES CONSISTENT WITH VISION

I recently had a conversation with a friend who is venturing into online dating, which is a ripe environment to examine vision, values, and consistency.

My friend is looking for a partner who is loving, smart, and open, someone who is authentic, honest, curious, and transparent. She seeks those values in the dating profiles of the men online. And she finds what she's looking for…in the profiles.

But when the men show up for a coffee date or a drink, the reality often is that they've lied about their age, or talk only about themselves, or are interested mostly in whether or not she can cook and if she likes football.

These men are perfect examples of people who live in The Drift and are not operating by a set of values consistent with vision unless that vision is to be inauthentic frauds or liars.

Here's another example. Let's say I'm the President, and I declare that I'm committed to bringing America together and unifying the country. But then five minutes later I say that Hillary Clinton and her supporters are losers. I've created a complete contradiction to my vision of unifying the country. True vision can't include those competing declarations.

If I'm a leader living by values consistent with my vision, I can't say that I'm going to create economic opportunities for everyone with a level playing field where everyone pays their fair share of taxes, and then turn around and create a tax program that is highly beneficial for the top one percent and does very little for the middle class and the poor. At that point, the vision, actions, and values through which I'm filtering my choices are totally out of alignment.

Mastering leadership depends on creating relationships based on values that are aligned with your vision personally and professionally. My son Nick recently got engaged, and from the moment I saw the Nick and Alex together, I thought they were perfect for each other. It wasn't about whether I liked her for him or not—although I did. It came down to the way in which they spoke and listened to each other. The level of respect and admiration between them was obvious and equal.

At the end of our first dinner, I called Hillary and said, "Nick's going to marry Alex." I knew it, I heard it, I saw it, I felt it. The values they shared were completely aligned with their vision and purpose.

Values are the pillars that hold up one's vision, and when those values are shared in relationship, the vision gains strength.

VISION VALUES VS. EGO VALUES

All of us operate through some version of values. The question is this: Who's choosing the values? Is The Drift choosing the values for me, or am I choosing them from my authentic vision as a leader?

Think of it this way. What gets you up in the morning? People get out of bed in the morning for lots of reasons. One of them is a vision. Another is duty, obligation, a long list of have-tos and to-dos.

When you have a vision, you jump out of bed because you're passionate about what you're creating. You're enrolled in it, you're committed to it, you're excited about it, and you want it to come alive. You're moving towards your purpose, and you see the vision and manifestation of it through everything in your life—your relationships, your family, your work, your activities, all of your choices. It's alive for you. If you're enrolled in and committed to the vision, you can't wait to get out of bed!

Now let's say you don't have a vision, but you have values, and one of those values is to keep your word and get up and go to work every morning at 8 a.m. You're going to get out of bed because you have a commitment to go to work, but that doesn't mean you're going to your job with a vision. Not everybody is living in vision; many people don't know what vision is and don't have a connection to it. Really. If you ask people what their vision is, a lot of them will say "20/20" or "I wear contacts."

Without vision, the question becomes how are you getting out of bed, and what version of you is getting out of bed? Are you getting out of bed as an angry, grumpy, tired, judgmental, sad, lonely victim? A 9-to-5 zombie? Is the version of you getting out of bed someone who lies on his dating profile? Are you getting out of bed as an egomaniac who's stirring up The Drift and perpetuating the thick, heavy current of mediocrity?

Ego has core values. Egomaniacs have core values. Being right, looking good, being in control, isolation, resignation, separateness, and scarcity are some of ego's core values. Ego can also look like victimization, excuses, justification, manipulation, and lying. Another form of ego is arrogance and feeling superior to others. Ego is being better and smarter than other people. But the true definition of ego is the separate, isolated self. Ego likes to keep us disconnected from each other and, sadly, disconnected from our authentic selves and our true possibilities.

Ego often shows up in people—even leaders—as lone wolf behavior. Lori R. Taylor is a motivational speaker, marketing & branding consultant, and entrepreneur who was named a "Top 50 Power Influencer" by Forbes two years in a row. She founded Rev Media, a social media agency in Cincinnati, and online pet food giant TruDog.

"I've always kind of viewed structure as a prison," she said, "and I've always liked to get things done the way I get them done. My dad used to say to me, 'you know, you're a great team player as long as you're the quarterback.' I've always resisted people telling me what to do because my way works."

Transformational leadership training with me showed Lori that her lone wolf behavior was influencing her team's results. "I didn't realize how my ways of being we're making it possible for other people to show up messy and creating havoc for the people trying to organize things. Lone-wolfing is more of a weakness than a strength, and it can create weakness on the team. You can't play team if you're a lone wolf, and rigor is a gift that can change your life if you use it effectively."

Vision's values are responsibility, integrity, authenticity; vision requires the highest level of commitment. Vision values your word, giving, connection, inspiration, win/win, honesty, excellence, communication, wisdom, grace, and character. When vision gets people out of bed in the morning, they're likely to declare something that is beautiful or powerful or profound or extraordinary; something that alters the course of history, the course of life.

Lori created an acronym for her core values. "LUCA" stands for love, unity, compassion, and authenticity, and it represents her vision for the world, which is to create emotional healing by raising consciousness.

"I show up every day with love, with a commitment to creating unity around me, bringing everyone together with compassion and authenticity. That's the way I can create emotional healing and raise the emotional intelligence of the people on the planet, to get them to see things from an ownership perspective rather than a victim perspective."

"SHHH" IS NOT A CORE VALUE OF VISION

We often operate from common limiting beliefs we learned in The Drift and rarely question them. How often have you heard this? "If you don't have anything nice to say, don't say anything at all." Well, of course, we all know that's true. Except it's not true. It's an ego-based limiting belief, and it's a huge player in perpetuating The Drift.

This adage is the biggest "Shhh" in The Drift. It orients us to be phony, to lie on our dating profiles, to withhold, to tell people what they want to hear. Untrue beliefs like this keep us from asking vision-driven questions of ourselves and others when something in our lives isn't working.

Leaders who live by values consistent with their vision are eager to ask transformational questions of themselves. Here's one: what's missing from me?

Have you ever been in a meeting with your boss or manager and she says, "Ok, team, I'd like to hear feedback from you. What's missing from me as your manager? What am I not doing that you need me to do? How am I showing up that isn't working for you? Please let me know because I want to change it."

How many CEO'S, executives, presidents, or leaders are willing to ask those open and honest questions? How many are willing to ask for honest and direct feedback? Not many, because it makes them uncomfortable, vulnerable, and opens them to the risk of embarrassment or not looking good. Imagine creating or working for an organization that is committed to honesty and vulnerability.

POWERFUL QUESTIONS + RIGOR = EXTRAORDINARY RESULTS

Master leaders are eager to routinely ask themselves and others rigorous questions that keep them credible. What do you see is holding me back? What's in the gap between where I am and achieving my vision? How do I reach the people I haven't been able to reach? Where do I need to go that I haven't gone before? What are the areas I need to develop or breakthrough? What skills or talents do I need to develop to cause or create something new or be more effective at causing my vision?

With practice, filtering your micro decisions and actions through your values —whether that action is to get a smile from the busy barista at Starbucks or to unify your project team—becomes a habit that gets extraordinary win/win results. It's a fundamental, essential aspect of applying this master leadership distinction in your everyday life. With practice, you'll start to see results. You'll start to be the cause of the change you want to see in the world.

Like anything else, you measure your effectiveness at creating and manifesting vision through results. Let's say I'm committed to creating my vision for peace, love, unity, and abundance in my family. How do I measure my results?

I know my daughter Savannah is showing up responsibly in her school work. She's doing well and getting the grades she wants, and she's performing at a high level of excellence. If she's working, earning money, is happy with herself, contributing to the family, empowered in how she feels about herself and how she's living, I'm going to consider myself effective at creating my vision in my family.

In business, you make results-based declarations for yearly, quarterly, monthly, weekly and daily goals and you measure them in a specific and tangible way.

With your vision, you dream, declare, and get to work. Now! You're committed and constant in your values. You set your benchmarks and begin to hit your declarations exactly as you said you would, or not.

And if not, you go back and ask yourself curious, compelling questions. What's working? What's not working? What's the breakdown? How and what do I need to do to shift it? What coaching do I need?

FILTERING DECISIONS THROUGH VALUES

Living my vision is the big picture, macro purpose of my life. On a day-in, day-out level I work as a trainer and coach. I am married, I have children, I have business partners, I have commitments. I have responsibilities. I have obligations. Like all of us, I have a myriad of tasks to complete every day. I use Distinction 3 as a way to filter decisions about those tasks and commitments through my values.

And I mean I filter everything through my values. For example, I recently needed to decide on a gift for an employee for her baby shower. My wife Hillary and I discussed it through a series of questions. Who is this employee to me? How much do I value her as an employee? How important is my relationship with her? How important is it to her (my employee) that I do something special for her? What would be the impact if I didn't get her a gift at all? I don't really have a personal relationship with her, but I do interact with her. She has a substantial job with significant responsibilities, and she's a valued employee who's worked with us and for us for two years. By the time we went through this process of filtering through my core values and vision, it made sense to me to get her an elegant gift. And that's what we did.

Here's another example of filtering decisions through values. A couple of days ago, I got a phone call from a student inquiring about hiring me as a coach. The reality is that it doesn't make sense for me to coach her; I'm out of her price range. I could have just said no, thanked her for thinking of me, and left it alone. But I didn't.

I applied the filtering process. Do I care about her as a person? Yes. Not only do I like her, but I respect her as a leader. Am I enrolled in her vision and commitment? Yes.

She asked if I could recommend other coaches. I said yes and told her I would support her in finding someone. I've trained and developed dozens and dozens of business coaches, personal coaches, and trainers all over the world, and I could have just put out a call for someone to jump in.

Instead, I filtered them through who would be the best fit for her given what she's up to and what she's looking for specifically. I worked with her as an unpaid partner and made three calls to three coaches who I trained and believe in, and who would see this as an exciting opportunity.

I put in the time to make those calls, to have the conversations, to create a win/win result. She selected a coach, and they have begun their business relationship.

I'm a busy man. I didn't have to do any of that. I did it because giving is one of my core values. Giving is consistent with my vision to create peace, unity, love, and abundance. It really came down to my desire to give. These are my friends. I want them to do well. I have lots of opportunities and more work than I can do. Why not take care of my friends and the people I love, admire and respect? It fills my heart to see them do well.

And if I'm committed to causing my vision to become reality, how am I going to do that by myself? How will that happen if I'm the only one doing it? It makes sense that I develop other people to be as good or better than me at what I do. Then I am sourcing, causing, and creating the critical mass that I believe will cause a rippling effect of transformation for the world. And it's happening, for sure, based on results.

**VALUES:
CREDIBILITY THROUGH RIGOR**

What are the filters you use in decision making? Where are you living consistently and inconsistently with your values?

_____

_____

_____

_____

_____

_____

_____

_____

_____

_____

What vision-driven questions are awaiting your answers?

_____

_____

_____

_____

_____

_____

_____

_____

_____

DISTINCTION 3 – VALUES

What are five core values that you will use to filter your choices and actions through, so you too, can manifest your vision?

_____

_____

_____

_____

_____

_____

_____

_____

_____

_____

Are you operating from vision-driven values or ego/Drift values? How and where can you shift into vision?

_____

_____

_____

_____

_____

_____

_____

_____

_____

DISTINCTION 4

ENROLLMENT: EVOKING AND AWAKENING THE VISION IN OTHERS

Enroll: to enlist, to sign up, to register.
Master Leader's definition: to inspire and empower another person to discover, bring alive and commit to their vision.

Mastery of leadership is a skill through which you understand the mechanisms, tools, and strategies that are effective in enrollment and leadership. When you're enrolling, you are inspiring and empowering people while leading them in the direction of your vision—and their own."
– Chris Hawker, co-founder, Next Level Trainings

Master leaders are inspirational and empowering, enrolling others in their vision. What makes master leaders stand out is their innate ability to share their vision in a clear and powerful way. Leaders empower the masses into movement, inspiring them to take hold of the vision as if it were their own.

Leaders who create the future don't do so by themselves. They are fully aware that visions don't typically happen without others to support the process. It takes a village to create visions that are worth having. The most significant accomplishments throughout history include countless people who had a role in their fulfillment. Nothing is quite as powerful as an idea whose time has come except for the group of people who give it life and the leaders who call that vision forth.

Over the last 30 years, I've asked thousands of people about enrollment. What is enrollment to you? When you hear the word "enrollment," what comes up for you? Most people will connect it with registration or recruitment of some kind, such as signing up for insurance or maybe a college enrollment application.

In the context of transformation, you must become a master enroller to be a master leader. Those most successful in personal and business relationships are expert enrollers. They are able to design their message, communicate it and bring their vision and message alive in a way that resonates and comes alive in other people.

When that message comes alive in other people, they are then able to see and take hold of the vision and apply it in their own lives. Their actions, choices, decisions, commitments, and behavior evolve as if it were their own idea from the beginning.

ENROLLMENT IS EXCITING AND AWE-INSPIRING

One of the greatest examples of a master enroller (and the one I use most often) is Martin Luther King, Jr. He often gets credit for the civil rights movement, yet if you rewind history and go back a bit further in time, it was Rosa Parks who actually sparked the civil rights movement with the 1955 Montgomery Bus Boycott in Montgomery, Alabama.

Local black leaders formed the Montgomery Improvement Association (MIA), enrolled MLK in becoming its president, and 13 months later the U.S. Supreme Court ruled segregation on public buses as unconstitutional. The bus boycott showed the power of nonviolent mass protest to create results and lasting change through mass enrollment in a vision.

Rosa Parks' refusal to give up her seat was a stand in The Drift and began the process of enrollment that led all the way to MLK. His vision, his dream to end racism and create civil and economic equality for all lives on 60+ years later. He is still shifting The Drift. He not only was, but I assert, still is a master enroller.

I know a lot about MLK. I've studied him for 30 years or more. I've read his books and books written about him. I've watched many of the movies made about him and his life. I've memorized his words and read and watched his speeches. I recently had the opportunity to watch a new documentary about him.

If I were on automatic pilot, if I were not standing up in The Drift, I could easily have said to myself, "I don't need to watch a documentary on MLK." I easily could have gone into "I know" mode, but I live the work of transformation and part of living the work of transformation is that I'm not attached to what I know. I'm not interested in being right about what I know. I'm excited about learning and growing and opening myself up to new possibilities. (Notice if you're starting to lose focus or interest at this point in the book because of what you think you "already know" about him.)

As I said, recently, I watched the new documentary about MLK and was completely immersed in being in the journey of discovering new information. I was present, watching as if I knew nothing about him, as if I was learning about him for the first time. I was fully enrolled in his words, his message, his music, the music behind the words, his facial expressions, the sweat on his brow. I listened as he delivered the "How Long? Not Long" speech given after the 1965 Selma march. This is an excerpt:

How long? Not long, because no lie can live forever.

How long? Not long, you shall reap what you sow.

How long? Not long...

How long? Not long, because the arc of the moral universe is long, but it bends toward justice.

MLK's words rang like a bell in my head, over and over. Talk about inspiration and evoking your vision in other people! Talk about enrolling people in a vision for themselves, for what's just and moral!

Three years later, King delivered his Mountaintop speech in Memphis, Tennessee where he said:

"Nothing would be more tragic than to stop at this point in Memphis. We've got to see it through. And when we have our march, you need to be there. If it means leaving work, if it means leaving school, be there. Be concerned about your brother. You may not be on strike. But either we go up together, or we go down together. Let us develop a kind of dangerous unselfishness."

Martin Luther King put himself and his very life on the line to achieve the dream he spoke about. He's been dead for 50 years and is still inspiring and enrolling others in his vision. He had a message for the world, and he shared it through his own creativity, unique voice and style, charisma, and emotional connectivity. Master leaders kinesthetically transmit their message and convey it to others in such a way that it almost has a life of its own.

Master enrollers enroll people in such a way that they understand a breakthrough is available in the vision the enroller sees for them. When we talk about leadership and the distinctions of leadership in terms of enrollment, it's about someone like me using myself, my vision, and my message to impact someone like you. To give you a jolt like a lightning bolt that lands at your feet and in your heart and wakes you up.

Enrollment sparks electric energy that compels you to act, to step boldly out of your comfort zone. To pick up a phone and call your mother and have the conversation you've been avoiding for ten or 20 years. Or finally move to start that business you've been talking about and procrastinating on, waiting until you know the universe and the stars align before you take action. Or to reach out to that former relationship you have not been able to forgive; not only so you can let them move forward in their lives and be empowered, but so that you can also set yourself free to act and engage and create the vision of what's possible for you in your own life.

Or, perhaps, as so many did who followed King's vision, to step into responsibility to create equal rights and stop racism—despite lunging dogs, fire hoses, risking the loss of life and arrest after arrest.

The life expectancy of enrolling others in a compelling vision—yours or someone else's—is infinite. Truly. When is Martin Luther King, Jr.'s vision going to stop or end? Sure, it's 50 years later, and some views and perspectives have changed. Are we completely transformed as a society? No. Is racism eradicated? No. Have we reached complete equality? No. But we're much closer. Fifty years from now, people will still be talking about Martin Luther King, Jr. He'll still be inspiring and enrolling others, as if he was still alive, as he does today.

Today his vision is alive in the "Times Up" and "Me Too" movements, the March for Our Lives movement, the West Virginia, Oklahoma, and Arizona teachers' strikes and many other modern leadership initiatives.

Anytime someone takes a stand in The Drift and enrolls another in social change and equality, Martin Luther King Jr.'s vision is alive. In a direct and profound way, he is still transforming the world and shifting The Drift.

VISION + ENROLLMENT = TRANSFORMATION

Enrollment is a never-ending, ongoing journey, and, like vision and transformation, it doesn't have a life of its own.

My vision for the world won't become a reality unless others are enrolled in it and take it on as their own. Remember, a vision grows and expands when it's shared with other people, resonates with other people, and comes alive within other people. When they choose to commit and declare the vision as their own, they are fully enrolled.

Vision, enrollment, and transformation are intertwined. Think of it this way: Vision + Enrollment = Transformation.

When I think of enrollment, I don't think of it as me getting you to join me in my cause. I think of it as me enrolling you to join you in your cause, for you to commit to your higher self, for you to commit to your higher consciousness, to commit yourself to evolve and transforming into your authentic self, the highest version of who you are.

Basically, I'm using myself as a vehicle to cause this impact and difference for you—which is much different than a manager in your office telling you what to do to achieve results for the company in order to keep your job. Enrollment is not "do it because I said so." That would be what I call "controllment."

For clarity, let's go back to Martin Luther King, Jr. In his book, *Stride Toward Freedom*, King said the real meaning of the Montgomery boycott was the power of growing self-respect among African Americans, which empowered them and gave life to change. King's vision for equality became a torch that passed from person to person, enrolling them in their visions of authenticity and consciousness, which led to transformation, to lasting change, and (perhaps eventually) to the full realization of King's dream.

Drew Canole uses this equation in his business. Drew is a sought-after personal coach, founder, and CEO of FitLife.tv, and the visionary behind online green juice company Organifi, which employs 140 people. His vision is to impact a billion people's lives through nutrition, making it convenient and accessible to the world.

"The vision is key; having everybody get the vision vs. just one man beating the drum and having people follow is what works. Everybody gets to beat the drum, and everybody gets to play a part in casting that vision out into the world."

Drew believes enrollment shifts The Drift.

"Enrollment is connecting to the individual in such a way that it's empowering for them to do something with you, together as one vs. being separate. I'm painting a picture for them of the vision they have for their life, and I'm enrolling them in the opportunity to rise up, to take a bigger stand, to impact more people, or to just play bigger, because a lot of people are sleeping. I think many people are just walking around like zombies endlessly roaming the earth. Enrollment wakes people up; I think of being enrolling as truly embracing the light that's inside of you and allowing it to shine, being the shiniest person in the room and not being afraid to put it all out there."

AUTHENTICITY IS ENROLLMENT MAGIC

Today, perhaps more so than at other time in history, we are suspicious of each other. Such phenomena as 24-hour, breaking-news driven media outlets, social media masks, and the perception that everyone has a self-serving agenda are on a relentless loop. They are served up with the intention to keep us in distrust and fear and keep us from switching channels or turning the tv off.

It makes sense. We're taught from a very early age that the world is out to get us. When we're young—still in that happy three-year-old stage—we know only what we're told, and what we're told is "Don't talk to strangers. Don't touch that. Don't do this. Are the doors locked? Where are you? Who are you with?" It's all about trying to control the horrible things that can happen to us in the world and The Drift that we live in.

Going back to the earlier building-the-box conversation, we create our comfort zone, which confines us within an imaginary space, and in that confinement is an illusion of protection. It's an ego-driven, identity-driven defense mechanism. We're taught to be skeptical of other people's intentions.

The Drift and the world continue to reinforce those limiting beliefs, and eventually, we don't know who to trust. We come to understand we can't trust anybody, really.

Trust issues are deep in The Drift. Remember, The Drift is ego-driven. It's concerned with looking good, being right, control, arrogance, judgment, selfishness.

Authenticity can't exist in The Drift, and the world is craving authenticity. Authenticity, which my friend Mary Jo Lorei defines as, "who I am when nobody's looking," doesn't have an agenda.

For example, when I'm out in the world, no matter what activity I'm up to, I practice living my vision on a micro level. Part of living that vision is being honest, playful, available, and kind.

I golfed recently with someone I've never played with before; he's a new member of my club. After 15 holes, he stopped and looked at me and in front of the other two players said, "Michael, I need to say something to you. You are the nicest person I've ever played golf with. I have never been complimented as much as I've been complimented by you in the time we've been playing. It's a real pleasure to golf with you." And I said, "Wow, that's really nice and thank you for saying that."

Now, I wasn't doing anything out of the "norm" for me. I didn't have any agenda to make him like me or impress him. I was simply being authentic, and my words reflected my experience of the person.

When your public and private conversations are aligned, you show up as authentic, and when people show up authentic, they have the power to move other people.

When Barack Obama spoke at the Democratic National Convention in 2004, suddenly everybody was talking about him. He was authentic in expressing his vision for America. Whether you're a Republican or a Democrat, it's hard to dispute Obama's authenticity.

When he gave a speech just hours after hearing about the Newtown shooting at, he stood in front of the entire world and cried as he talked about those kids. He was communicating authentically and from his heart, without any care or concern for what people would think of him for being vulnerable and expressing deep emotion. When Obama cried for those kids, many of us cried with him.

Enrollment really comes down to the authenticity of the vision, the authenticity of the message. If a message and vision move you, it's because you see the authenticity of the person delivering it. You get it because it's sincere. You get it because their intentions are to serve you, because they intend to empower you or to inspire you or to motivate you to go after what you want. Their authenticity has a way of diffusing your defensiveness, skepticism and trust issues.

I can tell when somebody has a hidden agenda, and many other people can, too. Often, though, people are too busy engaged in their own agenda to notice that someone else has an agenda.

When I'm in a training and I'm coaching, working, or present with somebody, I'm not thinking about anything else. I'm not on a different and unrelated agenda. I'm connected and vulnerable. I'm present. I'm here now. When I'm working with somebody to discover what their vision is, what they're committed to, I also ask them what's holding them back. I can always tell if they're authentic. If they're not, I'll work with them and coach them to shift out of whatever story or distraction might be holding them back so that they can move into authenticity.

When you take time to care about others and show your interest in them, that you're on their team and you're there for them, it makes them want more from you; they are more open and receptive to what you're offering them. They're inspired to enroll in the part of your vision that speaks to them authentically.

Enrollment has no end. The idea of enrollment, the idea of a vision coming alive so that it resonates within people and they bring it alive within themselves is like the passing of a torch. One person takes hold of it and moves it forward, shares it and brings it alive in others and so on and so on, like a rippling effect, until transformation happens.

This is how organizations transform, how families transform, how communities transform, and ultimately—if enough people are enrolled—how the world transforms.

**ENROLLMENT:
EVOKING AND AWAKENING
THE VISION IN OTHERS**

What does enrollment mean to you? Which transformational leaders inspire you?

_____

_____

_____

_____

_____

_____

_____

_____

How can you use the power of enrollment to bridge the gap between where you are now and where your vision becomes reality?

_____

_____

_____

_____

_____

_____

_____

_____

When are you most authentic? Are you the same person when you're alone as you are when you're in public? How can you be more authentic?

How will you use the Six Steps of Enrollment to evoke and awaken the vision in others? 1. Vision 2. Create Relationship/Partnership 3. Evoke vision in person 4. Advocate for the person's vision 5. Empower the person to take committed action; life is now! 6. Support and follow through with them.

DISTINCTION 5

CHANGE: ACCEPTING AND EMBRACING ALL FORMS

Change: to make the form, nature, content, future course, etc., of (something) different from what it is or from what it would be if left alone.

Master Leader's definition: to expect, accept, and embrace turbulence while being responsible for it. The power to alter circumstances and redesign or reinvent yourself in the face of them, without losing sight of your vision.

"Leaders are change masters. It's a rule of life. I don't wish that life was more predictable. It's the unpredictability of life that makes it fun."– Brad Ballard, co-founder, Ascension Leadership Academy

---

Master leaders are change masters. Many people spend their time wondering why things are the way they are, consumed only with what they see or hear. They are the spectators of life who only understand the obvious and who mistakenly think that all circumstances are the effect of some other phenomena or person.

In contrast, master leaders know that to achieve a vision people must find the ability to cause change within themselves first and then within others. While spectators get caught up in yesterday's news, leaders are thinking forward and letting go of the past. They instinctively know to accept and embrace what currently exists, then direct their energy to what is possible.

Many people figuratively rearrange the deck chairs on the Titanic; they appear to be making changes for the better, but the ship is still sinking. Master leaders, on the other hand, are change masters because they get to the heart of the problem and redesign how they operate in the face of that problem instead of hiding behind masks or pretending the problem doesn't exist. They are committed to creating an unprecedented future based on their vision and are continually reinventing themselves in the process.

THE DRIFT FEARS CHANGE

People don't like change. Why? Change is uncomfortable, and, when we feel uncomfortable, we often feel vulnerable. Sometimes we associate change with being wrong or bad, and it can produce tremendous fear and anxiety.

According to the 2018 World Happiness Report, the United States ranked #18 on the list of happiest countries in the world. Given that we live in the land of freedom and opportunity, I would think we'd rank much higher. We're not even in the top 10 of happiness? How is that possible? Perhaps we should focus on making America happy again!

Maybe people don't like change in America because complaining, griping, and judging are part of our culture. It's certainly true in the Drift. Many of us lock our car doors from the inside and drive around in our metal boxes, scowling with road rage, jockeying for position to get ahead of each other as fast as we can. And all of this so we can get to work, where we spend most of our awake hours and productive time in an unfulfilling job with a lot of other people who don't really want to be there either — including the boss.

We double-lock our doors. Think about how many locks the average person has in their house. It's a perfect metaphor for fear. We are living and surviving in a constant state of fear. We don't like discomfort. We don't like feeling vulnerable. As I made clear in Distinction 4, we have deeply ingrained trust issues.

We fear change. And the fear evokes out-of-control feelings that make us believe we have no power or authority over our lives. Allowing the fear to control us turns us into control freaks, not change masters.

Many people are on automatic pilot, in a constant state of "my way or the highway," rigid and fixed, settling for mediocrity, bored and complacent. Most people have expectations about the way they think things should be, or the way other people should behave, or the way someone else should think. As a society, we are attached to being right.

Of course, we want to control the outcome of everything in our lives. When we don't have control or things don't go the way we want them to go, we often react badly. Many of us go into desperation and survival mode and bury ourselves deeply in our comfort zones while we barricade the walls.

The idea of being a change master is surrendering and living in the flow. Most people are not in the flow. Most people resist the flow. The more they resist, the worse it gets.

MASTER LEADERS EMBRACE CHANGE

Change masters not only accept change; they embrace it, which is totally different. They embrace it as part of the experience of the daily game. They embrace change as part of the natural occurrence and flow of life.

When you're in the flow, you're prepared for change; even when you don't know what change is on the horizon or what it looks like, you know change is coming.

Let's look at change from a business perspective. Those businesses that are most successful over time embrace change. They realize that whatever is working will continue to work until it doesn't. Eventually, what's working will stop working. No matter what business you're in, an idea will come along that will disrupt business in some way, be more effective or efficient, or costs less.

When change hits, most companies are not prepared for it. In 30 years of training and coaching people and businesses, I've seen major havoc created when companies are unprepared for change. The inability to embrace change, to lead it and get out in front of it, causes companies to fail and go out of business.

Think back to the housing market and Wall Street breakdowns that led to the economic crisis in 2008. As George W. Bush pushed home ownership (shortly after September 11, 2001) and bankers sold sub-prime mortgages, the country continued to buy and flip homes and invest in real estate. The failure of industry and government leaders to anticipate (and in some cases leaders willfully ignore) the warning signs of a failed housing bubble created a severe economic downturn that impacted global politics and economics.

Master leaders understand that the nature of business and the economy is that it changes. Master leaders anticipate that shifts will occur and get out in front of them. Smart companies build change into their growth strategies.

One of my clients is a couple who own a small business with 14 employees. The company is flourishing, and they want to grow the business substantially, which means bringing on more people.

We recently had a conversation about what's working and not working in the company, and it was clear to me that they're not on the same page; they have different views on the way company growth can or should develop. They care about each other, respect each other, and want to work together, but if they fail to get on the same page, the lack of alignment on how to address the challenges are likely to undermine their success.

I suggested they create a clear and powerful vision and get to work enrolling the current staff, top to bottom. As they move forward with a hiring strategy for the company's growth, they commit to bringing in people who are enrolled in the vision, and who operate from the values and distinctions of leadership, rather than hiring based only on qualifications or education only, which is what most companies do and where they make tremendous mistakes.

Apple is a fantastic example of a company that lives in the context of embracing change. Every August, the tech world starts salivating and speculating about what Apple will release in the fall. The company embraces change and also creates a demand for it. With Tim Cook at the helm, the company is reinvesting in America. Experts estimate Apple's direct contribution to the US economy will add up to more than $350 billion over the next five years. That's master leadership.

Jennifer Sconyers is president and founder of Abundance Leadership Consulting, and creator of Culture Shift by ALC, a program designed to shift an organization's culture by creating awareness and choice and sustainable behavioral change. "My vision is that we are actively building intentional communities where people are seen, respected and heard," she said.

Jennifer's career includes past work in political institutions in Washington DC, Maryland, and Ohio. Part of her professional focus is on developing other leaders, and her reaction to the 2016 U.S. presidential election required her to shift her thinking, to reinvent her relationship with change.

"The day after the election I had a real moment of reckoning, and it was all because up until then I had thought that if we have the right people in office, with the right policies and organizing strategies, we would see change in my lifetime. I realized that if I'm not going to see those results, it is now even more important to impact change by developing other leaders, so I can pass the proverbial torch on to the next generation. If we do that, we will eventually see a shift."

EMBRACING CHANGE RESULTS IN CHANGE

Master leaders incorporate and facilitate change at home as well as in the workplace. Anybody who has been a parent for more than ten minutes knows change is inevitable. Parenting is not a perfect science.

My wife Hillary and I have three kids at home who are 17, 15, and 13. We recently had a conversation about each of them and college. Are we going to cover all of their college expenses or create an arrangement to share the cost with them? It's not that we can't pay for their schooling, but a shared payment arrangement will serve to create personal responsibility for their education and facilitate their transition from teenagers to adults.

Hillary and I are engaged in that conversation now even though we're two years away from the first one going to college. We expect breakdowns; we expect change to happen. We don't expect the process to work the same way for each child. We don't expect entirely smooth sailing along the way. We embrace the turbulence; we immerse ourselves in the responsibility that will guide them and us through the commotion. Embracing change means we're not surprised when the turbulence happens.

We're proactively preparing for future conversations in the present and preparing our kids to embrace change as well. When the children in our society think money grows on trees, when their every need is met, they can begin to build a conversation that anything and everything they want always comes "to" them. But it came to them because it was provided for them by mom and dad.

When that person is 18 or 20 or 22, their expectation can become, "I always get what I want. I don't have to work for it."

Collectively, are we preparing our kids to be future leaders? No. Are we preparing them to learn how to be ready for the curveballs and challenges? No. When we give our kids everything, we are perpetuating The Drift. They tend to get stuck on a metaphorical one-dimensional track and create an interpretation of life that everything must fit on that track. If it doesn't fit on that track, then it doesn't work. At that point, it's a consumer track, not a leadership track.

It is possible to prepare our kids for leadership and to be flexible and responsible in the ways they interpret life so that they have access to any and all possibilities. When we're responsible for it, we have the power to alter the circumstances or redesign or reinvent ourselves in the face of change.

CHANGE IS EVOLUTION

The idea of change is gradual, the gradual movement from one responsibility to another, from one context to another. Master leaders are committed to reinventing and redesigning themselves in response to new challenges and new endeavors, or in response to circumstances beyond their control.

In most companies, people are typically promoted because they excelled at their previous job, not because they're skilled at leadership. They bring the same ways of being, the same attitudes, the same personality to the new role and the new position.

One of my favorite examples of this is Magic Johnson. After the three-time NBA MVP retired from the Los Angeles Lakers in 1991, he returned briefly as head coach at the end of the 1993-1994 season. He quit after three weeks. The team finished the season on a ten-game losing streak, and Johnson's final record as head coach was 5–11.

When Johnson's good friend Larry Bird was asked by reporters why he thought Johnson quit, he said it was because Magic still thought he was the best player on the team. If you break that down, what was Bird saying? He was saying that Magic was unwilling to change his ways of being—his context, his operating style, his communication.

Magic didn't understand that leadership isn't about him. It's about inspiring other people to achieve results. It's about coaching or evoking other people to be better than you are at what you do. For Magic Johnson, making that change from being a player to a coach was a completely different dynamic. At that time, he wasn't ready for change.

CHANGE CAN BE EMOTIONAL AND TRANSFORMATIONAL

Not all of us are superstar basketball players, but challenging dynamics at work are common for most of us. What happens when a master leader—or someone on their way to becoming a master leader—works for a boss who won't or can't embrace change, whose ways of being are not in alignment with the vision?

I call that situation managing your manager. It requires learning to empower and inspire upward, and it demands confidence in yourself, courage, honesty, and personal integrity. With courage, you do everything you can to empower your manager, to inspire your manager, to manage your leader or boss to get on board with the vision, to really embody the vision.

When you've turned yourself inside out, and it doesn't work, I believe that your personal integrity and fulfilling your vision and purpose in life must become more important to you than staying in that situation. If not, your vision will die a little bit every day.

I found myself in a similar dilemma years ago. I was in a leadership position with a company I was deeply committed to and sadly, saw inevitable, dire-straits change coming. I didn't believe the company could survive such fatal change.

After many meetings, phone calls and direct, interruptive, honest conversations with my boss, I exhausted every possibility to empower him to see the possibilities. He couldn't see it. In my view, my only choice was to leave and pursue my vision, become an entrepreneur and start my own business. Change sometimes looks like being willing to blow up a relationship or let go of the status quo in order to stay committed to your vision. Ultimately, the breakdown can actually lead to a whole new world of possibilities.

Embracing that type of change is rarely easy. But my vision of transformation for the world, for what's possible for people, was and is unwavering. What shifted was the mechanism, the vehicle that I was using to achieve it.

Accepting and embracing change also means allowing whatever comes up in the process. For me, it was the feelings of sadness, grief, anger, frustration, and fear. I was invested in my dreams and what was possible for the company. I experienced lots of tears and sadness, as well as second-guessing the decision to leave.

I went through all of those emotions, but I didn't stay in them. As a master leader, while I was allowing myself to experience my experience, I was also simultaneously taking action to pursue the vision and make my new business a success. I opened my coaching company, Direct Impact, and doubled my income the first year.

Everybody has a certain level of emotional intelligence, a certain level of intuition, relationship skills, sensitivity, vulnerability. Everybody has some understanding about their ability to relate or connect with the world around them, their place in the world, what they can cause, what they can create in challenging situations. But not everybody has it at a heightened level like a master leader.

Master leaders display and evoke emotional intelligence. They have their hand on their own pulse, on the pulse of the organization and its beating hearts—the people and players involved, the championship team they are inspiring to manifest the vision. When leaders don't feel and express genuine, heartfelt emotion and real PASSION, a key ingredient is missing in their commitment to master leadership.

Master leaders have a healthy relationship with change. Change masters think about the future today, ground for the future today, and prepare for a conversation that will happen at some point.

Accepting and embracing change is essential in sports, in business, in relationships, in family and ourselves, so that everyone is on the same page and working together to cause the vision all are committed to creating.

**CHANGE:
ACCEPTING AND EMBRACING
ALL FORMS**

Do you fear change? If so, why?

_____

_____

_____

_____

_____

_____

_____

_____

_____

What would be possible for if you let go of control and fear?

_____

_____

_____

_____

_____

_____

_____

_____

_____

Where are you resisting change?

Given your vision, which attitudes and ways of being will you need to adopt to implement change?

DISTINCTION 6

RISK-TAKING: SHAMELESS COURAGE

Risk-taking: the act of exposing oneself to the chance of injury or loss; a hazard or dangerous chance
Master Leader's definition: the act of being bold, daring and vulnerable. To take a stand for something that is uncomfortable and matters, regardless of fear, history, or evidence to the contrary.

"To get out of The Drift, you've got to take action, take a risk and do whatever it takes."– Margo Majdi, founder, Mastery in Transformational Training (MITT)

Master leaders are risk-takers. Risking is woven into the fabric of every significant vision throughout history. It requires the ability to transcend fear and operate at full capacity without having any answers or guarantees toward the result. For leaders, risking is being vulnerable to their vision and commitment, which exposes them to criticism, disapproval, and even failure.

Although fear is a pervasive and powerful motivator, leaders are completely willing to give up their comfort zones and face their fears head-on. Their relationship with fear is unique because leaders use their own fear as motivation, challenge and, most of all, opportunity. They see value in taking risks and experiencing the emotions that go with risking because they understand that to achieve truly extraordinary visions one must go where no one else has gone before.

RISK AND MASTER LEADERSHIP

After 32 years in this work, what I know is that the world is full of wonderful people, good people, great people, amazing people! The world is full of people who want permission to let others into their lives, who want to open their hearts, who want to be connected, who want to come out and play, who want to be their authentic selves. And A) they don't know how; B) they're in fear; and/or C) they're waiting for permission.

What it takes to cut through the fear, invite others in, and interrupt The Drift is commitment to risk-taking and shameless courage.

In the context of risk and master leadership, leaders don't wait for permission; they don't wait for someone else to give them power. Leaders don't procrastinate. Leaders don't wait for someone to notice them. Leaders don't suffer in scarcity, disconnection, loneliness, sadness, and emptiness, merely existing and settling for a mediocre experience of living. Leaders find within themselves the courage to find their voice and use that voice to stand up and shamelessly commit to their vision.

Risk-taking is taking a stand in the face of all evidence against it, taking a stand in the face of no evidence to support it, taking a stand without a net, where there may or may not be support for them. Risk-taking is taking a stand anyway because your vision and your commitment to that vision propels you to do whatever it takes, and what it takes is courage.

What it takes is shameless commitment—meaning it matters more to cause the vision, to create what's possible for yourself and the world than it is for you to get approval or permission or settle for being right about "the way it's always been."

The Drift is risk-averse; taking a stand requires leaders to transcend fear, to leap toward courage.

RISK IN THE DRIFT

The Drift trains us to choose comfort over risk. The antithesis of risk is fear. Choosing to risk, especially without certainty of survival, and inviting the danger of emotional, mental or physical pain, is terrifying to most people.

In The Drift, we learn to fear in much the same way we learn to build our comfort zones: a repeated pattern of events that create interpretations that in turn, create beliefs.

Most fear is learned fear. On a cultural level, it begins when we first start school, where we're acclimated to society. In the early years, we're "graded" on politeness or creativity or how well we play with others. We're still discovering who we are, learning our place in the world. Ideally, in those years we're in a constant state of discovery, adventure, wonder, and love, and we're all one. We sing and play, and we experience little disconnection or separation.

As we get older and start developing and acclimating, we begin to adapt and take on ways of being as well as certain assumptions about ourselves and the world. And then the world starts to point things out about us that challenge those assumptions.

As an example, let's say you're age six or seven and all the kids are on the playground at recess picking a team for kickball. But they don't pick you. Nobody wants you on the team. This could be your first realization that you're not like everybody else, or you're not good enough, or you're being singled out. It could be the first time you tell yourself that there must be something wrong with you.

That moment could be benign. Maybe you're just a crappy kickball player. The fact that you didn't get picked might not be personal at all. After all, the purpose of the game is to win, so we pick our best team and best athletes. But the way it goes down, either because of the way the message is delivered, or because of the way the other kids react to it, or the way you interpret it, you begin to question yourself. You're unable to make the distinction between "I'm not a great athlete" or "I'm a poor kickball player" and instead interpret it as "I'm being singled out" or "nobody likes me" or "I'm bad, wrong, worthless, not good enough."

What I'm describing is a button event that activates a response inside a person that causes them to invent an interpretation, point of view, or belief that leaves them feeling as if they're wrong, beaten down, defeated. It creates a trigger, and when that trigger is pulled that person retreats backward deeper into the box, into the comfort zone. And it's a pattern that all of us experience, over and over in life.

Someone else may interpret that same experience a different way. My brother Larry and I are close in age; he's a year older than I am. Larry would have seen such an event as an opportunity to say, "I'll show them," or "watch me prove them wrong."

But I interpreted those moments as evidence that I should pull back, retreat, be afraid, walk on eggshells. I learned that it was safer to pretend to be somebody else, and, in my teen years, I became a master at the art of pretending, so I could survive and get the things I wanted—attention from a girl, popularity or a place on the team.

Inside I was having panic attacks of worthlessness, yet I was able to get beyond them and cause results. My interpretation held me back from risking, from taking action, speaking up, stepping out, taking a stand, running for student council. I wanted to run for student council, but I didn't run because I was afraid of hearing the feedback that I already believed about myself. My feedback to myself was that I didn't matter. I didn't want the whole world to know that, so what did I do? I became the class clown because that's a role I felt I could win. It was in my wheelhouse.

I would take risks by being sarcastic or inauthentic. I would make people laugh to get them to like me. It was my survival tactic.

Most kids go through this conditioning, and many get indoctrinated in the tribalism of school society. They start to separate and sort into groups—the nerds, the jocks, the cool kids, the hipsters, the mean girls. These pockets of people gravitate towards each other and build subcultures inside of the culture. It begins in middle school and gets bigger and more pervasive in high school.

Tribalism grows in adulthood; we self-sort into our safe groups based on politics, race, economics, and career. We fall into and live by the fear habits we've learned from our parents, our families, our authority figures, schools, society, the media. "Don't do this." "Don't do that." Human beings are domesticated, indoctrinated, and encultured into a world of "DON'T." It teaches us that we are limited, that if we stay in our boxes, in our comfort zones, we'll be happy, and we'll get everything we want. Or, at the very least, we'll get through life. We'll survive.

Is it any wonder we—in our collective society in The Drift—are risk averse?

RISK IS LIFE

When we look deeply at what's under our fears, we often find survival at the root of them. You may have heard this acronym for F.E.A.R.: False Evidence Appearing Real.

Let's take roller-coaster rides as an example. Some people love them; they're driven by the thrill and the adrenaline rush they get from the ride. But a lot of people won't get on a roller coaster, and, if you ask them what they're afraid of, they'll say "heights."

What they're really focused on is the fear, and what's under that is death. They've created an illusion that if they don't get on the rollercoaster, they won't die. Humans invent and tell themselves many such illusory stories. "If I get a tummy tuck, somehow that's going to stop aging." "If I get a facelift, people won't know how old I am, and I'll live longer." "If I get my penis enlarged, my boobs lifted, get the fat sucked out of me, get this sculpted and that manicured, I can avoid the fact that I'm aging and falling apart, that I'm not what I used to be, that I'm going to DIE."

The sad part is most of us don't truly experience LIFE as adults. What we experience is survival and what we settle for is a mediocre experience. Because we fear risk. We avoid the climb of the rollercoaster up the gigantic hill, the uncomfortable feeling in the pit of our stomachs as it begins, the clacking of the car on the track as it climbs to the top. Because we know that when we reach the peak, the ride is going to throw us down the incline and we can't do a damn thing about it.

Sometimes we transcend that initial fear (false evidence appearing real) of "I could die here," and when the ride is over, we want to do it again and again! Why? Because, for those brief minutes, we transformed our relationship with fear and found courage, and instead of holding back and playing small, became a risk-taker.

When we're in the middle of it, flooded with dopamine and adrenaline, we're shameless, screaming as if we're releasing a lifetime of pent-up fear. For a few minutes on that ride, we don't care how we look; we don't care what people think. We're fully in the experience and shamelessly committed to the risk. When we are in that exhilaration, that joy, we want to do it again and again.

The roller coaster is a metaphor for life. Master leaders choose life, choose exhilaration, choose risk and shameless courage. When we are risking, we are truly ALIVE.

Truly ALIVE leaders like Preston Smiles understand the value of risk and its potential for impact. Preston is the best-selling author of *LOVE LOUDER: 33 Ways to Amplify Your Life.*

"Learning to take risks has been a game changer in my life. My capacity to sidestep the conversation that would have had me sticking close to home where it's comfortable is now expanded. I think that all of us have medicine in our hearts that only we can give to the planet.

"I would be doing humanity a disservice by playing small and staying on the sidelines, getting ready to get ready. People are suffering and dying every day with their medicine—with their dance—still inside them. And it's important that I, among many others, reach the corners of the world I can reach with what's on my heart, to remind people of their truth."

SHAMELESS COURAGE

Fear and courage are a two-headed coin. When we feel fear, the focus is inward, and the energy of it is retreat, protectionism—human bubble wrap. But flip that coin over to courage, and the focus is outward. The energy created is excitement, passion, freedom, exhilaration.

Shameless courage means that you're unbridled. You're untethered. You're out on the skinny branches of the tree, inventing and creating while completely at risk and vulnerable to the vision you're standing for.

What is the ultimate opportunity for being human? It depends on who you ask. If you ask a master leader, if you ask someone in transformation, they'll say the ultimate opportunity is to create a vision and a purpose that drives your life. If you ask a typical person who lives in The Drift, they're going to say the ultimate opportunity is to be in control, to be stable, to survive.

Master leaders are not concerned with control and stability. Master leaders thrive on instability and lack of control. They don't worry about having it all together. They are committed to life being profound and rich. They're standing for what's possible, and they're transforming and evolving into the next level of possibility in their life. They don't sell out. They don't care about being right. They're constantly creating something new.

Most humans in survival context in The Drift are information gatherers, imitators who suck up and soak up what others create. I believe everybody longs to reconnect with who they truly are; an inventor, a creator, a visionary who knows the juice in life lies in creating something that wasn't going to happen anyway.

And you cannot do that without courage, without risk-taking, without shameless commitment. When you're shamelessly committed, you embody the vision. It's in your blood, and you don't give a flying you-know-what about what people think. That is a powerful place to be.

Stepping into your shamelessness takes courage, but it doesn't mean you must run head-on into the road without looking. It begins by taking daily action that forwards your vision.

Let's say you're at work in a brainstorming meeting and you're burning with a brilliant idea. You're excited! You believe your brainchild could ignite and take the company to a whole new level. But you know your idea could be shot down, which is why you haven't shared it.

Isn't this your opportunity to be a risk-taker? Your opportunity to be shameless? Even if you're tempted to be passive and quiet and play safe, you step into risk and take ownership and leadership. You present your idea with conviction and power and confidence and depth, and you don't back down to scrutiny and worries about what everyone else is thinking. When you're clear on your vision, you take the risk.

Learning to risk is a skill, and it's especially important in the workplace. Corporate America often models a culture of inauthenticity and hierarchy that discourages risk and shameless courage.

Brad Ballard is the co-founder of Ascension Leadership Academy in San Diego and an effectiveness and leadership coach who specializes in facilitating workshops and trainings for corporations. He also coaches and mentors owners of real estate companies and financial service franchises.

"Most of the private clients I coach are CEO's and entrepreneurs, and I support them in creating a culture of real relationships in business," Brad says, noting that he coaches them to move away from traditional working relationships and toward relationships that work based on shared vision. "What would happen if everyone at work with a shared vision dropped their walls and dropped into intimacy and vulnerability? When that's created in the workplace, companies take things to the next level."

Brad believes our current buttoned-up "never let 'em see you sweat" workplace environments are a lose/lose for both company and employee. "It's why turnover is so high in the workplace. You know, if people think they can't screw up, can't take risks, can't apply their own unique passions and skill sets, they become cogs. And when people feel like they're not human and they're just a cog in the machine, their whole vision walks out the door, and we know what happens when vision dies. It doesn't work."

Risk-taking in your personal life is a learned skill as well. If you're a single person, how do you create relationship possibilities? Are you going out and saying hello or sitting home waiting for your soul mate to show up on Match or Bumble? If you live in Boston and you're at home six nights a week, is it because there's nothing to do in Boston, or is it because you're hiding and playing small, rather than taking risks and being shameless about it?

If you're a shamelessly committed and courageous master leader in your own life, you take action by going out. To Starbucks, a bookstore, a museum, a restaurant, the park. You get social, and you go where people gather, and, when you see somebody you're attracted to you say, "Hi!" You don't stand over on the sidelines with your fingers crossed, hoping they'll notice you.

Sometimes an event shifts people into risk, and they find their vision and the courage to stand up in The Drift. The students at Marjory Stoneman Douglas High School are a prime example. After the mass shooting on Valentine's Day in 2018, these teens found the courage to speak up, to be leaders, to create an interruption in the public conversation, and do whatever they could to get their voices heard.

It took the shooting for it to happen, yet, when I listen to them speak, it's as if they were born for this; like they've been prepping for it for their entire young lives. They're taking on the status quo, taking on the legal system, but they're doing it with such eloquence and grace and confidence and clarity and depth of knowledge that it tells me that if this level of leadership is possible for them, it's possible for all. It took the shooting to bring it out. And that makes me wonder how many people in America are like them. This is just one high school in one town; imagine the possibilities if more young leaders stepped into such empowerment!

Master leadership can inspire people to rise up BEFORE the event, so that leadership like this comes alive on a one-on-one level, on a family level, on a friend level, on a school level, on a community level, on a global level. By being willing to risk, we can create a wildfire of leadership and vision that creates a shift in The Drift, despite the evidence against it.

RISK-TAKING:
SHAMELESS COURAGE

Name three risks that you are committed to taking that will transform, breakthrough or take your personal and professional life to a new level?

_____

_____

_____

_____

_____

_____

_____

_____

_____

_____

_____

What new actions can you take daily to develop your risk-taking skills?

_____

_____

_____

_____

_____

_____

_____

_____

_____

_____

What would be possible if you transcended the fears of risk-taking that holds you back?

If you were shamelessly committed to your vision and shifting The Drift, what actions would you take today?

DISTINCTION 7

RESPONSIBILITY: PAST, PRESENT, AND FUTURE

Responsibility: the state or fact of having a duty to deal with something or of having control over someone.

Master Leader's definition: the state of being the sole uncontested author of your life; to stand as the cause and source of everything, including your past, present, and future.

"Mastery of leadership means that I stand in a place of total 100 percent responsibility in my life. It's a practice of choosing—moment to moment—to stand as the source. If it's going to be, it's up to me." – Ivette Rodriguez, author and transformational coach

---

Master leaders are responsible for it all. To be responsible is to be the sole, uncontested author of one's life. Leadership is responsibility in action. Leaders do not expect someone or something else to cause their vision to become reality. Leaders are responsible for it all: from the concept to the implementation to the final result. To master leaders, the obstacles and pitfalls that occur along the way are merely challenges that make the ride all the more enjoyable and valuable.

Many people become victims to the problems that arise on their journey towards a goal. The result is usually failure. Being responsible means being free and inventing and originating solutions to problems and new visions for achievement. Responsibility is not a burden, duty, or obligation, but an opportunity that includes a sense of ownership and power.

YOU ARE THE SOURCE

What's missing from our current collective interpretation of responsibility—the state or fact of having a duty to deal with something or of having control over someone—is the aspect of source.

In the context of mastery of leadership, and inherent in the concept of responsibility, is the understanding that you are the source. You are the cause. You are the sole uncontested author of your life. You are the cause of the past, the present, and the future.

When you experience yourself as the cause, you have the power to impact yesterday, today, and tomorrow. You have the power to choose how you interact with all aspects of your life. You choose what to do with it or what to create with it—whatever it is.

Most people do not associate creativity with responsibility, but the essence of responsibility is creativity. When you are responsible, you are accessing your inventiveness and ingenuity to generate the life, experience, relationship, job, transformation, possibility—whatever it is you're committed to creating.

Master leaders know—and are excited by the knowing—that they are 100% responsible for everything in their lives, including their results, health, success, income, fitness, and the quality of their relationships.

MASTER LEADERS ARE RESPONSIBLE FOR IT ALL

If you ask the typical American, "Are you responsible for Donald Trump being president?" they'll say "yes" if they voted for him and "no" if they didn't. The people who didn't vote for Trump—even those who did not vote at all—will claim that they absolutely are not responsible for him being in office. The people that voted for him, of course, will claim responsibility because they touched the lever and through their actions made Donald Trump president.

From a Drift perspective, we understand that we're responsible for something as long as we can touch it, see it, control it. Most of us are unable to see how we're responsible for something that's happening on the other side of the world, or how we're responsible for something we had nothing "to do" with.

In the context of master leadership, however, the concept of responsibility goes far beyond what we can touch.

I did not vote for Donald Trump, but I can see how I am responsible for his being president. Operating from the context that I am responsible for it all gives me the opportunity to look at what I could have done to impact the outcome of the 2016 presidential election.

What difference could I have made that I didn't make? How many people did I register to vote? How many people did I proactively support in voting? What could I have done to support non-voters to get them to the polls? Young adults are the smallest voting block in America. How many 18-to-25-year-olds did I personally persuade to vote?

If I had taken action—if I had spent time, if I had reached out, if I had called everyone in my network with kids between those ages (and that's thousands of people)–I could have directly impacted the vote. I didn't do any of that. That's how I see my responsibility for Donald Trump's election to the presidency.

My friend and colleague Ivette Rodriguez is a transformational trainer, coach, and author in Puerto Rico. Ivette uses the illustration of school shootings to explain her interpretation of being responsible for something she didn't create.

"I can stand as the source of some maniac shooting kids in a school—not because I caused that maniac to go and shoot kids in a school—but because I can identify with it. When I stand as the source, it's doesn't mean I'm guilty of what happened," Ivette says. "For example, there are always red flags before something like that, and standing as the source can show me where in my life I am sometimes indifferent to red flags around me. I become more aware. I truly believe if we all stood in that place of awareness and responsibility, we'd be living on another planet. We wouldn't be pointing so many fingers."

Master leaders choose responsibility as enlightened human beings who make conscious decisions to be aware and responsible for every facet of their lives, whether those decisions involve their personal lives or their lives as global citizens of the planet.

RESPONSIBILITY IN THE DRIFT

In The Drift, the idea of accepting responsibility for something one didn't directly create is a hard sell.

Society often uses shame and blame to guilt its way out of accepting responsibility. The Drift likes to blame the world for its problems and point fingers to explain away lack of accountability. Shame: "I'll never get promoted because the boss doesn't like me. Shame on him." Blame: "I failed my finals because the questions were too hard. That teacher is out to get me."

In the Drift, responsibility is commonly interpreted as obligation or duty.

Often when people say, "I am responsible," what they actually mean is, "Fine, I admit it, I did something wrong. I messed up. You can blame me because it's my fault."

This version of responsibility occurs after the fact and there often is a stubborn reluctance associated with it. I am reminded of Donald Trump's comments at a rally in Wisconsin after authorities intercepted bombs sent to a variety of prominent Democrats he regularly disparages. In response to requests that he tone down his rhetoric, Trump told the crowd, "And by the way, do you see how nice I'm behaving tonight? Have you ever seen this? We're all behaving very well."

Responsibility is not something that's applied to a situation after some transgression happens. Responsibility is built into the operational context of interpretation and choice.

The Drift teaches us that accepting responsibility is an admission of guilt. If we accept responsibility, we're at fault. Not true. Responsibility is not synonymous with fault and blame.

For example, because of the nature of my work, I travel frequently. When a flight is delayed and causes me to be late, I am not to blame. I am not at fault for the delayed flight. However, regardless of the breakdown with the flight, I am 100% responsible for being on time to the business meeting and responsible for the consequences if I am not.

RESPONSIBILITY VS. VICTIM

In the context of master leadership, if you have to "take" responsibility for something, then you weren't responsible in the first place. You're a victim.

The Drift engages with life from a victim perspective. It conditions us to blame something or someone outside of ourselves for our circumstances, failures, all the stuff of life we're unhappy about. We blame our parents, the government, our spouses, the boss, anyone but the one person who is responsible — the one in the mirror.

Let's use a pinball game as an easy analogy to illustrate responsibility vs. victim. Can you picture a pinball game? If you're responsible, you're the paddle. If you're a victim, you're the ball.

When you're the ball in a pinball game, you have absolutely no power, influence, or authority over what happens to you. You are at the whim of the paddle and at the mercy of whatever objects and holes it throws you into. You are ruled by happenstance. People who live in victim mentality are controlled by the demands of others. They tend to ask, "why me?" and are unwilling to become actual owners of their lives.

Think of people in your life who are late all the time and eventually show up with a story about why it's not their fault. That's victim mentality. Victims tend to procrastinate, hang out with people who won't hold them accountable, gossip, live in the past, make excuses, and are angry at the world.

Living in victim mode is a choice, and as soon as you choose it, it takes your power. You give your power away to whoever you believe is victimizing you.

All of us experience the role of victim at some point. If you've ever felt powerless, were treated unfairly, decided that you had no control over anything, that the world was out to get you, that you couldn't do anything right, you've been in victim mentality.

Think about the last time you were stuck in traffic, crawling along the highway. Did you automatically shift into victim mentality? Many of us do. Victim in traffic sounds like this: "Why is this happening to me? I can't believe these people! Why do they let old people drive, anyway?"

Road rage is a symptom of our collective victim mentality. We are a nation of angry drivers, which results in frustration, anger, and resentment. We tailgate, yell obscenities out our windows, flip each other the bird.

A 2014 study by the AAA Foundation for Traffic Safety says more than 78% of U.S. drivers reported having engaged in at least one aggressive driving behavior one or more times during the previous year. It reminds me of the movie "Groundhog Day," when Bill Murray's character says to Phil the Groundhog, "Don't drive angry!"

In our society, we're constantly looking outside ourselves to find joy, empowerment, bliss, happiness. We don't realize that we are keeping ourselves in the mentality of victim, that we ourselves are generating the lack of experience we're looking for, and that we ourselves can transform our relationship with our lives and transform our relationship with living by accessing responsibility.

Do you find yourself looking outside of yourself for your self-worth? How often do you feel overwhelmed and stressed out financially and blame it on money problems, issues, obligations? What if your issue with money wasn't about money at all, but in fact is actually about your RELATIONSHIP with money? If you feel like you don't have the power in your relationship with money, you're creating a victim experience.

One of the lessons Hillary and I are working on with my seventeen-year-old step-son Andrew is teaching him to create a responsible relationship with money. He has a quarterly allowance for his chores, and a budget. At the end of each month, Hillary sits down with him to see how effective he's been in managing his money. This is an invaluable lesson as he matures into adulthood. He's truly learning the value of money, choices, prices, and ultimately financial responsibility.

I work with people all the time who value money more than they value vision and happiness. Many people confuse happiness with money, so they chase it like crazy. No matter how much they have, they want or think they need more.

Many others—and I see this consistently in my trainings—value themselves even less, and they struggle in a victim mentality of scarcity. I'm sure you're familiar with the expression "robbing Peter to pay Paul" which is a perfect example of the loop of scarcity. Perhaps you or someone close to you is suffering and continuously living in lack and making spending decision based on either/or. That's a relationship breakdown with money.

Think of victim as a sieve, or a tire with a slow leak. Imagine changing your relationship with money and stepping into responsibility in a way that your self-worth doesn't have anything to do with your net worth.

Many of our heroes and inspirational influences from history share the commonality of being in deeply distressed situations—from slavery to incarceration, to confronting the various forms of The Drift of the day—and using those situations to design their lives from the power of choice.

Jackie Robinson, the first African American to play in major league baseball in the modern era, could easily have given up when faced with racism, judgment, and threats against himself and his family. He could have given in by becoming a victim, laying low and passing up his dreams. But instead of lashing out or selling out, he rose up and chose responsibility by taking the high ground in the low-lying mud that was prevalent in the MLB and America. Jackie Robinson led with responsibility and did it with grace and professionalism.

Imagine what would change in the world if we all shifted from victim to responsibility.

Many of our heroes and inspirational influences from history share the commonality of being in deeply distressed situations—from slavery to incarceration, to confronting the various forms of The Drift of the day—and using those situations to design their lives from the power of choice.

Jackie Robinson, the first African American to play in major league baseball in the modern era, could easily have given up when faced with racism, judgment, and threats against himself and his family. He could have given in by becoming a victim, laying low and passing up his dreams. But instead of lashing out or selling out, he rose up and chose responsibility by taking the high ground in the low-lying mud that was prevalent in the MLB and America. Jackie Robinson led with responsibility and did it with grace and professionalism.

Imagine what would change in the world if we all shifted from victim to responsibility.

IF IT'S TO BE, IT'S UP TO ME

It's not possible to build anything of value from a victim mentality. There is no place for victim in vision, and the only alternative to responsibility is victim. There is no "kind-of" responsible.

One of the ways master leaders begin to stand up in The Drift through the distinction of responsibility is by taking a close look at where they're operating from to begin with and then reviewing their results. The questions then become "what's working" and "what's not working?" Where does the mentality of victim show up in your life? What are the prices you pay for being a victim?

With the awareness generated from those answers, you can start to connect with the conversations, the attitudes, the behaviors, and the limiting beliefs that are getting in your way.

When you're responsible, you take action and create momentum. Responsibility in action begins with replacing your internal beliefs that you are a victim in any way, that you have no power to create change, that you can't do something because you're not good enough. When you believe someone else (he, she it, they, the boss, the man) is keeping you down or preventing something from happening in your life, you've given up your power and are in a victim conversation, which will produce the results and experiences consistent with being a victim.

When you shift those beliefs, let them go and move into responsibility and source, you have the power to create anything you declare. To act from responsibility is to begin to bridge the gap between where you are and where you want to be, or between the current result you have, and the life results you want.

Master leaders create from within the context of responsibility. Creating in an organization where the paradigm is responsibility gives you and the organization the power to create the experience in an environment conducive and consistent with the intended vision.

And it's all up to you. If responsibility means you are the source, the sole uncontested author of your life, then who do you need to talk to in order to empower yourself or your team? Yourself!

My friend Quddus created tremendous success early in life as the host of MTV's "Total Request Live." After a couple of projects failed around 2011, he found his way to transformational leadership training through his friend Preston Smiles.

"That was my first taste of great experiential training, and it was really powerful," he said. "I went from one training to the next for a couple of years because I was experiencing so much growth. Within a year I also experienced the resurgence of my career and got my first actual primetime network hosting job with a show called "Duets," a singing competition show on ABC."

Recently Quddus and his wife Carmina Becerra founded Camera Ready, an experiential media training company. With a new business, he's stepped into a heightened relationship with the distinction of responsibility.

"There's a lot to be responsible for when you're running a company and facilitating trainings where there are so many variables. It's easy to go to some level of victimhood around all of the things that can happen on any given day at any given training, so it's been a really beautiful thing to ask myself how I can respond creatively in an empowered way to challenges. I'm able to rise to the occasion when I have that frame on things, and it constantly expands who I think I am when I'm responsible for whatever is occurring, rather than collapsing into some blame or shame game about it."

Like Quddus, you can create an internal dialogue that shifts you out of those limiting beliefs and victim conversations into seeing and embracing the opportunity of responsibility. When you see that opportunity and act upon it, you spark momentum — powerful, fun, exciting momentum! The rallying cry, "If it's to be, it's up to me!" generates energy, action, and behavior, which in turn generates a shift that creates fresh results.

When you see and experience those results, you want more of them. Think of responsibility as, "I go to the party and I am the life of the party I go to." Think of victim as "I go to the party and hope that it's fun. I go to the party and hope that somebody talks to me. I go to the party and hope that somebody else generates the good time I'm looking for."

If you're responsible for it all, who's generating the good time? You. If you're responsible for it all, who's generating the love in your marriage? You. If you're responsible for it all, who's leading the company? You. If you're responsible for it all, who's recognizing and acting upon filling the gap to get you from where you are to the success you've declared in your vision? You, of course!

Responsibility gives you the power to create what you want vs. going through life like the ball in a pinball game, waiting for one of the paddles to whack you into the light where the bells go off.

Everybody wants the bells and whistles to go off in life! Where does that experience come from? That experience comes from responsibility. When you are responsible, you have power. When you have power, how do you feel? When you are responsible, you are the author of your life. When you're the author of your life, how you feel? Like you can do anything! Like you can create anything!

In the Drift, responsibility looks and feels heavy, guilty and resentful, and we're passing that down to our kids. I don't know about you, but when I was a kid, there were very few adult role models that I wanted to emulate. Not because of what they "did or didn't do," but more because of their behavior.

Even now, most adults seem to be stressed out and unhappy. Many—with the exception of a few—are disconnected, sad, beaten down, self-righteous, arrogant, cold, boring and not fun.

John Mellencamp said it best in "Authority Song" with the lyrics "growing up leads to growing old and then to dying. And dying to me doesn't sound like all that much fun!" The first time I heard the song when I was about 18, I thought the purpose of life was to mature into a "responsible" adult. I resisted it hard. "Please no! Make it stop!"

Through transformation, I understand that responsibility is a gift. No matter what The Drift has taught you, when you're a master leader living your vision from the context of responsibility, you act with the joyful freedom of a child, with youthful exuberance.

Creating joy and fun and freedom demands action! I recently took my wife Hillary to a U2 concert. What's a rock-and-roll concert about? Youth! Passion! Vision! Inspiration! Dancing and singing! Celebrating life and living!

Over the past summer, I went body-surfing with my family. How many other 53-year-old dads did I see on the beach? Very few. How many other middle-aged husbands and wives did I see out body-surfing with their families? None!

What do kids do at the beach? They make sand castles. They splash and swim in the water; they play frisbee and volleyball; they simply play! I do all of those things, and I do them with Hillary and the kids. The kids see and experience adults who are happy, fun, and engaged in life, and who are operating from responsibility.

Living from responsibility gives you the power to stand up in The Drift when you declare, "I am the sole uncontested author of my life. If it's to be, it's up to me!"

**RESPONSIBILITY:
PAST, PRESENT AND FUTURE**

Which areas of your life are you feeling powerless, like a victim?

_____
_____
_____
_____
_____
_____
_____
_____
_____
_____

How can you change your view of the situation and apply the distinction of responsibility?

_____
_____
_____
_____
_____
_____
_____
_____
_____

DISTINCTION 7 – RESPONSIBILITY

In what areas of your life are you responsible for outcomes that you did not directly create?

_____

_____

_____

_____

_____

_____

_____

_____

_____

_____

Now that you are the author and cause of your life, what will you create with the power of responsibility?

_____

_____

_____

_____

_____

_____

_____

_____

_____

_____

DISTINCTION 8

COMMUNICATION: WORDS, MUSIC, AND THE ART OF LISTENING

Communication: the imparting or exchanging of information.
Master Leader's definition: to deliver your message in a profoundly impactful way.

"Connection and communication are about being real, being authentic, listening compassionately and understanding, not judging or dismissing people." – Natalie Jill, founder, owner, and CEO of Natalie Jill Fitness

---

Master leaders are expert communicators. Communication is a two-way street. True leaders understand that to master communication they must listen as well as they speak. They realize that they were born with two eyes, two ears, and one mouth for a reason. By using all of their senses, they can connect with their environment whether it is one person or one million people.

A leader's effective communication is directly related to what has first been communicated to them in various forms. With a clear picture of what's needed, master leaders are exceptional at speaking and presenting concepts and ideas so that other people truly understand. Master leaders are not interested in merely saying what they want to say but are instead committed to communicating a message that stirs the emotions of their audience and at the same time provides an understanding of usable, relevant information.

COMMUNICATION IS ART

What passes for communication in The Drift is static. Twitter sets the news agenda for the day. People are more intimately connected to updating their Snap Chat, Facebook and Instagram status than they are with their families. We can't take our eyes off our phones. A recently published paper in the *Journal of Applied Psychology* identified a phenomenon called 'phubbing,' which means snubbing others for your phone!

The Drift bombards us with "communication" that is actually a form of advertising and attempts to influence the ways we think, buy, and vote. What passes for communication in The Drift is in many ways manipulation, a selling of distrust. It has become a duplicitous game to keep us guessing about who and what is behind our messaging.

In the context of master leadership, communication truly is an art form. Master leaders are accomplished communicators, which means they focus on far more than their message; they are focused on their vision for what is possible for their audience. Moreover, expert communication includes the art of listening. Committing to a vision and communicating it with impact relies on both speaking and listening.

Essentially, mastery of leadership is having and committing to a vision, being responsible for and communicating the vision, and, of course, impacting and enrolling people in the vision. Delivering your vision effectively is about flexibility and adapting your ways of communication including your ability to connect with the listening styles, personality styles, and the ways of being of the people in your audience.

To truly communicate your vision masterfully, you must bring your intention alive in the listener. You must bring it alive in such a way that the listener is so connected and empowered by the vision, the message, or the possibilities you're communicating that they take hold of it as if it is their own.

TRANSFORMATIONAL COMMUNICATION

In my work as a transformational trainer, I communicate from the front of the room for ten or twelve hours a day in seminars that can last four to five consecutive days. I do it without notes from a place of high energy and excitement. I've been doing it for 30+ years, and it never gets old! How is that possible?

It's possible because I'm communicating through vision! I'm using my vision to inspire my students and clients to see possibility, to create their own visions. I'm transmitting information that is in my mind, yes. And, of course, it's in my bones and my body because I live the context and distinctions of the content that I'm delivering. And I am also able to invent and create new ideas on the fly, shifting as I determine what each audience and situation calls for in the moment.

In the first few days of working with a student or a client, I'm coaching them to see the vision. I'm coaching them to let go of their ego and limiting beliefs so that they can see that vision, so they can work with it commit to it and ultimately embrace it. Then what almost magically happens through that work is they begin standing up and talking about their vision with power and passion, with a deep sense of ownership as if they always had it! And when they're doing that, that's when I know, as a trainer and a coach, that I'm doing my job.

The ability of a master leader to speak in a way that impacts people, touches them, or moves them in ways that evoke something meaningful has everything to do with their ways of being in general and also with Distinction 7, which is responsibility.

Master communicators are responsible for, are at cause for, and are the source for landing the message they intend to land. The communicator, rather than the listener, is responsible for making sure the listener "gets it," to identify what works with and doesn't work with the audience. It's an art form that requires the ability to speak, to listen, and to absorb the ways of being, listening and attitudes, and the wants and needs of the people receiving the message.

If my audience is sitting there nodding their heads and agreeing with me, that's my clue that I am not responsibly delivering my message. Simple agreement with my message doesn't further my vision, or theirs. Agreement doesn't mean I've made any difference in my listener's life.

When someone is nodding and agreeing with me, I stop and ask any number of questions, such as: "Besides agreeing or disagreeing with me, what's opening up for you?" "What possibilities do you see?" "What are you getting out of this coaching or distinction?" "What are you absorbing?" "What's landing for you?" "What's being evoked in you that you can use to create your vision, to create a life worth living?" "What do you hear that will cause you to create a breakthrough in your relationship or career?" "What are you hearing that will create transformation in you to become a leader in the community or world in the ways you've always wanted?"

Once my audience or my client begins to recognize that my message is about them, that I'm inviting them to look deeply into exploring and investigating the vision possible in their lives, I begin to see that light bulb, that "ping!" go off for them. When they have a glimpse of their vision and are excited to share it with others, I know I've expertly delivered my message. Expert communication occurs when people "get it" for themselves.

MOTIVATION VS. TRANSFORMATION

Motivational speakers are in the business of helping people learn about themselves, motivate career growth, and change habits. They provide tremendous energy, information, and conceptual communication to their audiences.

I'll use Tony Robbins as an example because he has a huge following. People love him and are motivated by him. When you ask people who have attended his events what they thought of the experience, they'll say, "I loved it. Tony's amazing and great!"

It's my experience that motivational events are largely about the speaker and results for the audience aren't necessarily long-term. It's challenging for people to create lasting results with the takeaways provided through motivation as a stand-alone tool.

I think of motivation as external. People are often motivated to attend an event or buy a product by the celebrity of the speaker, by their "brand," by the popularity of their message and the marketing buzz around it.

I think of inspiration as internal; Wayne Dyer called inspiration "in-spirit" as a way to describe the flow state that happens when we are creating and living authentically. Motivation and inspiration are not the same as mastering leadership and transformation. Transformation changes lives, often permanently. Transformation requires continual realignment with vision.

Thus, the key to measuring effectiveness as a master leader and expert communicator is through the lens of what your audience or clients are saying and creating in long-term tangible and measurable results. This is especially true when they are connected to something they learned that they are using in their everyday personal and professional lives.

What's the lasting change? Where's the transformation that follows the motivation? What are they creating three months, six months, or 12 months after the experience?

What are they saying about themselves? How are they living their lives? What new actions are they taking to move them toward their vision? What breakthroughs are they generating in their relationships, their businesses, their finances?

For master leaders, expert communication focuses on the person on the other end of the communication. It is focused on the receiver.

I know I have communicated at the level of a master leader when my student and clients walk away from our shared experience fired up about themselves and their vision and are fully empowered to use the tools they've received to enhance their lives and the lives of others.

THE ART OF LISTENING

In The Drift, most people listen like robots; there's no generosity and often very little humanity in the listening. They're in an internal conversation during the listening, often asking themselves something like, "How long do I have to pretend to care about this, so he'll stop talking to me? Hurry up! I don't have time for this."

In Drift communication, the listener is often paying attention to a host of things: unrelated wandering thoughts, disconnection, perhaps making up a story such as, "What does this have to do with me? This is not about me, ugh, it's boring."

They also may be judging the communication, judging the information that's coming in, judging the person that's speaking. They may be thinking, "Oh, I like this person." Or, "I don't like this person."

Many listeners are intent on finding a point to disagree with, as if they have a checklist in their heads while someone is speaking. Their thoughts are following along as they listen: "Okay." "Yes, I get that." "Uh-huh." "Yes." "Yes." And then: "No!" That person is listening for something to argue about, often so they can be right or feel the need to make you wrong.

Other people listen to respond, and you'll know that's their listening habit when they use terms like this (I know you've heard this one): "I know." "I KNOW! "I knoowww." Oh, I know." "Now, let me tell you about me and my experience." First, they're listening is like a broken record, playing the same note over and over again. Second, they're selfishly listening for a way to turn the conversation back to them, or for an opening to one-up the speaker. Is that truly listening?

Here's another term you'll hear when people are listening to respond or let you know they agree with you. "Right?" "Right." "Yes, right." Or they combine them. "I know, right?" That's not listening. That's someone publicly announcing that they're judging everything that's coming out of your mouth. When that happens, you may feel like you're talking to yourself. How often do you feel like the person or people you're talking to are just not getting it? Not really listening?

In the context of mastering leadership, listening is not just hearing words, responding to words, and reacting to words. Listening is the art of getting the intention behind the communication and addressing the intention and the underlying thoughts, feelings, emotions, and motives of the communication.

When people feel listened to and heard, and they feel like you're "getting" it, it means you're "getting" them, and they in return will be open to you and receptive to your message. Listening makes people feel cared about, and when people feel cared about, you're actually in relationship with them.

Whether I'm in front of an audience training or coaching someone individually, I'm completely immersed in the other person. Immersive generous listening is also an art. When I'm listening generously, I'm engaging this way: What is she saying? What is her purpose in her communication? How does she feel?

123

What's her experience? What's her message to me? What does she want me to hear?

If you and I are having a conversation, I'm transparent with you. I'm not focused on my thoughts and my feelings. I'm immersed in you. When I'm coaching or training, I'm generously listening to you. I'm listening to what matters to you, what your dream is, what your vision is for your life.

Most people don't think in terms of vision, and, when I ask them about their vision, they'll tell me a story about their life. What I'm listening to as they're speaking are their words and what those words reveal about the speaker. Where are they operating from? Who do I need to be or what do I need to do in order to partner with this person so that they can move into their vision as a concept, and then become or reinvent themselves into the person that will make that vision real?

THE MUSIC IN COMMUNICATION

When I'm in front of an audience, I'm speaking to everyone in the audience. I might be in Dallas or Puerto Rico or Mexico or California or New York. Culture matters; my tone of voice matters. I vary the rhythm of my speech, the words I use, the examples and analogies I give, all based on who's in my audience.

People are the music in the art of communication. After more than 30 years in this work, I now hear that music almost effortlessly.

I haven't always been able to do this, of course. Becoming a master expert communicator takes persistence and practice. As in any practice or sport, when I first started out, I worked at it every day. Every single day—practicing, coaching people, living the work, understanding the distinctions, understanding the distinctions more deeply, understanding the nuances of the distinctions.

And from there learning how to communicate those distinctions to the person I'm working with or the person I'm coaching.

Learning the nuances of how to communicate with different people requires rigor and real selflessness. People are infinitely unique in the ways they speak and listen.

How do I communicate the value of commitment? How do I communicate the value of honoring your word? How do I communicate the possibility and power of vision in someone's life in a way that resonates with various personality styles and cultures and motivations? How do I deliver it in a way that they can take hold of vision and step into it and own it for themselves? It's practice and repetition day in and day out.

Over time, through thousands of different experiences, I would have light bulbs go off in my head, and I could actually observe and listen to a person and know how the conversation was going to go before I spoke. Eventually, I could look at people and read them without conversation. It's not about judging a book by its cover; it's about putting myself in their shoes and adapting to connect.

Now, they often don't have to say a word to tell me about themselves. I can tell who someone is by their body language, facial expression, by the way they dress, walk, talk, carry themselves. I can read a person by their physical body posture, how they say "hello." I can often tell who's in a relationship, who's not in a relationship. I can certainly tell who's happy. I can tell who's disconnected and lonely. I can tell if somebody lacks passion or joy. I can tell if somebody has a chip on their shoulder or if they're arrogant and judgmental. I can tell if somebody is insecure and has low self-esteem.

I can look at people, read them, and be connected with them in such a way that I can imagine what life is like from inside their body. I now trust my experience of the person to tell me how to interact with them.

Over the years I've had thousands of people—complete strangers—say this to me: "How did you know that? How did you know that about me? You read my mind."

At times when I'm in the training room, and while a student is speaking, I'll turn to one of the interns sitting next to me and say, "This person will say the following words next...," and the person says those exact words. I'm listening to their inner voice, and I can hear what it's saying because I'm transparent, I'm connected, and I'm immersing myself in listening.

Master leaders immerse themselves in their audience. They don't just talk sideways over the people in the crowd or to the closest face smiling up at them. They connect with the entire audience, and they're able to design, redesign, and reinvent their communication to land it with the audience. They generate feedback along the way to be able to gauge if their message is working or not working. If it's not working, they adjust.

I can't tell you how many times I have had to do a 180 because I realized in the middle of training or a coaching session that I was doing a fantastic job coaching myself or providing amazing coaching for one person out of 100 people in the audience.

When I realize that what I'm doing isn't working—by being transparent and listening to the inner voices through feedback— I identify that a shift needs to take place. I adapt to it, shift into it, and boom! The magic happens; transformation happens, and visions come alive.

That's where mastery of leadership is an art, and new levels of communication are continuously available to us. Learning how to self-correct, how to hear yourself, and see how you're showing up in the room while you're in the room is an art. It's the music.

And that experience is possible for everybody.

AUTHENTIC COMMUNICATION

Sometimes when people speak—including prominent leaders—their words metaphorically drop out of their mouth and fall flat at their feet. Such speakers don't connect with their audiences, and, when they don't connect, the audience can get fidgety, bored, sleepy, distracted.

Many leaders have one pitch, and that pitch works for some audiences and not for others. Donald Trump has a pitch. He throws out that pitch over and over and over again. It works well for those who support him. It doesn't work for the people who don't share his perspective.

I could make the same point about Barack Obama. I believe Obama is an expert communicator. When he was running for president, and while he was in office, he often altered his pitch and conveyed a broader message to all Americans. When he did, his effectiveness and approval ratings rose.

Sometimes Obama lectured. Sometimes he was funny; sometimes he was incredibly vulnerable. Sometimes he was analytical and deep in the ways he expressed himself. At times he was complicated, or loud and firm, or soft and persuasive. He varied his pitch based on what the situation and audience called for from him.

President Trump seems to have only one pitch. If he wants to get beyond his current base, to connect with more Americans, he'll have to change it. Trump will need to shift how he communicates, show vulnerability, sensitivity, empathy, thoughtfulness, and consistency. He'll need to identify that he can't talk to kids and tell them how much he cares about them and that he's working to make schools safer and then a couple of days later be the keynote speaker for the National Rifle Association.

Those kinds of inconsistencies resonate with the people who are skeptical of his intentions and create distrust.

Authenticity creates trust. Authentic communication is when one's public conversation and one's private conversation are aligned. Authentic communication happens when the words that are coming out of one's mouth and their private internal, non-spoken words are the same. That is the power of authenticity, and master leaders communicate with authenticity.

When a leader says the words, "Believe me..." or "To be honest...." How do we react? I react with suspicion. If someone asks me to believe them, I suspect a lack of authenticity. I feel like I'm being sold something, and I question their motives. Why is this person selling me over and over again? What kind of a person is this? Is it somebody who is genuine or disingenuous? Is this person honest or dishonest?

When a leader speaks authentically, I don't suspect them of ulterior motives or hidden agendas.

THE BUSINESS OF COMMUNICATION

In the context of the business world, authentic communication and generous listening are virtually nonexistent.

It's rare for a manager to sit down with an employee and listen to discover their true vision and purpose in life. It's rare for a manager or business leader to evoke that vision and connect it with a company vision. It's not in the management handbook.

What IS in the management handbook is control and dictate. The manager dictates to the employee what he or she needs to do for the company, to keep his or her job, or to raise the bottom line. A manager talking to a subordinate is not leadership.

But it could be. Imagine what would happen in your company if inspiration and empowerment replaced control and dictate.

Our Drift definition of control in the workplace is someone — your boss or team lead — finding a way to get you to do what they want you to do — whether you want to do it or not is irrelevant.

Inspire and empower, on the other hand, is someone evoking in you the possibility stepping into action and seeing the value of doing it in such a way that you're enrolled in it, that you're on board with it. Ultimately, you are empowered to accomplish it.

It is possible to manage through coaching and partnership, evoking the attitudes and ways of being and commitment necessary for employees to take on an idea as if it were their own. Consequently, the manager or the boss becomes the wind in their sails.

Vulnerable and transparent communication is also not common in the Drift's workplaces. How often have you seen your boss or the leader of your company redesign himself or herself during a speech or presentation because they realize what they're doing isn't working?

Probably not often, because it's rare for someone to stand in front of the room and say, "Okay, clearly I'm not being effective in communicating the vision and message I'm trying to get across to you. So, please give me feedback right now. Let me know what's missing so we can shift it, and I will shift it right here on a dime. I'll shift it because I'm committed more to the success of this organization than I am to looking good and being right. Please feel free to speak up."

Can you imagine working for that leader? Don't you want to BE that leader? Wouldn't you like to have what you say resonate for people so much that they run out of your meeting, excited to step into the vision and own it as if they thought of it, and not to get away from you? That's the value of master leadership.

THE POWER OF COMMUNICATION

Michelle Stann is a former student of mine who is deeply dedicated to the work of transformation. She is a lighting designer and theatre professional in Hollywood. Michelle describes herself this way: "I'm what we call a hundred-footer. That means you can tell I'm gay from 100 feet away. So automatically, walking through life, I experience judgments and assumptions upon first glance."

Michelle's definition of mastery of leadership is based in the instant silent feedback she receives about her appearance. "Mastery of leadership means I can walk into a room full of evangelical Christians and still be effective in my message of leadership and love no matter what judgment I'm facing. It means that I can walk into a room of right-wing Republicans and still be effective in communicating connection and love. To stand in my power such that people still get my message is mastery."

Tracy Austin is a student who came into my life briefly and changed me forever. Tracy graduated from the Breakthrough training at Next Level Trainings in Columbus, Ohio, in October of 2016 and died from pancreatic cancer in 2017. I dedicated this book to him.

I will never forget Tracy's face at his graduation. That memory is in the top one percent of experiences I've ever had with a student at graduation, and it happened right before he was diagnosed with cancer.

Tracy came up to me, laughing and giggling uncontrollably like a child, like a little boy! How often do you see a 55-year-old educated man, who is respected in his community and respected in his business, laughing and hugging and vulnerably expressing his love, his appreciation, his gratitude?

Tracy's behavior expertly communicated his experience. He didn't come to me and say, "Michael Strasner, thank you. You're very good at your job." If he had, I would have thanked him and moved on. Instead, I walked away from him saying, "Wow!" This is a completely different man from the man who walked into this training four days ago. He's transformed in the ways he's showing up, his communication, his leadership and the way he's expressing himself.

I called my wife Hillary that night and told her about Tracy. I do trainings like this two or three times a month and meet hundreds of thousands of people every year. It's rare that I call Hillary to tell her about a specific person. But in this case, I had to share about Tracy. I was compelled to share. Hillary now knows Tracy, without having actually met him.

That's how expert communication happens. I made an impact in Tracy's life. I evoked something in him. He then evoked something in me. And I then evoked something in my wife. And that's how mastery of leadership happens. It's speaking, causing, creating, and being the source of landing your communication.

We have the power to cause change every time we open our mouths. And when we do, we powerfully shift The Drift.

**COMMUNICATION:
WORDS, MUSIC AND THE ART
OF LISTENING**

What will it take for you to become an expert communicator?

How impactful and effective are you at speaking? Listening? How
do you know?

What would your business partners, families, and co-workers say about your communication skills?

_____

_____

_____

_____

_____

_____

_____

_____

_____

_____

_____

What does authentic communication mean to you?

_____

_____

_____

_____

_____

_____

_____

_____

_____

_____

_____

_____

DISTINCTION 9

OBSTACLES: HURDLES ARE OPPORTUNITIES

Obstacle: something that obstructs or hinders progress.
Master Leader's definition: a challenging invitation, an opportunity to rise up and achieve in the face of doubt and uncertainty.

"Without obstacles and opportunities, you will never know what kind of leader you can be." – Mike Bacile, owner, The Daily Java

---

aster leaders see all obstacles as opportunities. Obstacles are an inherent part of any significant achievement. The circumstances of life are constantly changing, and new developments in people, places and things can cause difficulties to arise at any point in time. Master leaders are not only aware of this, but they also know how to anticipate the obstacles to which ordinary people make themselves victims. This anticipation of the

135

unknown makes it easier for leaders to stay on task and reach their goals, but this distinction goes much further.

Master leaders persevere to find workable solutions in every situation, even when most people would throw in the towel. They are steadfast and driven with unshakeable intention and focus and are grateful for the opportunity that comes with any challenge.

Master leaders maintain perspective. They realize that circumstances are rarely as bad as they may seem. They somehow see through the chaos that exists around them without becoming chaotic, and they find a way to rise above the unfamiliar hurdles of life on their path to accomplishment.

THE ONLY WAY IS UP THE MOUNTAIN

In the context of master leadership, vision always guides. When leaders are committed, connected to and embodying their vision, when they're deeply rooted in the vision, when it's in their heart and body and soul and spirit, they have access to infinite possibilities. No circumstance or obstacle is greater than that vision.

Sometimes the only way is up the mountain—literally.

In May of 2018, Xia Boyu, a native of China's Qinghai province, triumphed in his dream to summit the peak of Mt. Everest. It was his fourth attempt. His first attempt in 1975 took his feet. At that time, he and his team were almost to the summit, but weather forced them to descend, and, when one of his teammates lost his sleeping bag, Xia offered his. Severe frostbite from that trip required the amputation of both of his feet.

Both of Xia's legs were amputated below the knees 20 years later due to lymphoma. On artificial limbs, he tried again to summit the mountain in 2014 (a ridge of ice collapsed, killing 16 climbers), 2015 (an earthquake), and 2016 (weather again stopped the climb).

At 70, from the hospital where he recuperated after finally achieving his vision, Xia told *TIME Magazine*, "I failed to conquer it four times over the past 40 years. But because of my perseverance and effort, Everest eventually accepted me."

I imagine what Xia told himself is some version of "I'm climbing to the top of Mount Everest. It might have taken my legs, but Everest is not taking my vision. I'm not giving in to the circumstances of this obstacle."

When a master leader has a vision they are committed to, embodying, and immersed in, they live from a level of commitment, creativity, and resourcefulness that invites a never-ending possibility of solutions to bridge the gap between where they are and where they want to be or where they are and the completion of that vision.

Whatever their obstacle is, master leaders don't let the mountain take their vision.

EMBRACING ANY AND ALL OBSTACLES AS OPPORTUNITIES

Xia stuck to his vision through breakdown after breakdown after breakdown. A breakdown in the context of master leadership is just what it sounds like. Plans, ideas, and strategies fail. In essence, failure starts at the beginning.

Though it might seem counter-intuitive, Xia created a breakdown in his vision to climb Everest simply by declaring it. Because even before he lost his limbs, he had no evidence he could achieve that vision.

Leaders know they have a breakdown the moment they declare themselves a leader. When someone declares themselves a leader and declares a vision to cause or create something, they declare that eventually, they will create results consistent with their vision.

The moment a leader declares a vision, a breakdown occurs. Their results are already inconsistent with the vision. The breakdown is that the vision hasn't happened yet. There are no results.

To stand as the source of the vision and declare results without evidence requires that the leader accepts the challenges that go with the vision they declared. They accept and embrace any and all potential obstacles that come with it. With every obstacle, master leaders have the opportunity to resist it or embrace it.

Embracing it means tapping into creativity, into resourcefulness, redesign, reinvention. When a leader has a vision, they're not attached to how it manifests. When a leader has a vision, their only attachment is to the outcome; to creating the experience, the transformation, and the results. A vision is not an expectation, and some people confuse the distinction between the two. Expectation comes from a judgment of what "should be." Vision comes from a declaration of what "could be."

Think of business leaders who have visions to declare new products, new services, new ways of delivering those products and services. Of course, they experience countless obstacles. Where are we going to come up with the money for this? How are we going to allot the time? Who's going to lead this project? Does this person have the qualifications? Countless questions, actions, and processing go into the creation and fulfillment of the new vision.

Every time a new iPhone model is released, the technology experts in the industry give their opinions on what works and what doesn't work with it. Those reports usually run either in advance or immediately after the product comes out. Apple receives the feedback, and they immediately know what's missing and what they need to fix, correct, or shift about the NEXT product even though they just released the new one!

Today we rely on our phones to function, but 60 years ago technology like hand-held computers and rocket ships were little more than pictures in comic books.

In a 1961 speech to Congress, President John F. Kennedy announced his plan to put a man on the moon by the end of the decade. Except he had no plan. At the time, the U.S. couldn't even get a rocket off the launch pad. The technology didn't exist. No clear strategies, policies or procedures existed.

Kennedy's vision was essentially science fiction. Until it became reality. Kennedy's declaration became truth on July 20, 1969 — before the end of the decade, as he had envisioned — when Apollo 11 commander Neil Armstrong stepped off the Lunar Module's ladder and onto the Moon's surface.

It took infinite breakdowns and obstacles — including the deaths of three Apollo 1 astronauts who died during a preflight test — to get a man on the moon. It took repeatedly addressing the breakdowns and obstacles in resourceful, creative, ingenious ways to invent and reinvent technology, to invent and reinvent the plan. And that is how any business becomes successful and how any leader manifests their vision.

NAYSAYERS IN THE DRIFT

Not everyone was enrolled in Kennedy's vision. Polls from the 1960's consistently showed voter resistance to space program spending.

Of course, naysayers are always happy to criticize vision and dreams. That's the nature of The Drift. The Drift is full of mediocrity and people who are settling for ordinary, or who don't or won't believe in possibility because they're not vision-driven. They've given up and resigned themselves to "My life is pretty much the way it is, and there's nothing I can do about it. I'm a victim. I'm a victim of circumstance, a victim of my environment, a victim of my boss, a victim of the government. I'm a victim of people not getting how wonderful I am."

The Drift also is full of people that are out to discredit and tear down and judge and reject and ridicule anything that might change the course of life or possibility. The Drift doesn't like it when acceptable "knowns" turn into unknowns.

Barack Obama's presidency was a disruption in The Drift and created tremendous discomfort for some people in the United States, as evidenced by the level of overt racism and anger that resulted from it. His presidency still pushes the buttons in many people's thoughts, interpretations and social media posts!

Master leaders with unprecedented, unimaginable visions naturally push those buttons. Anything that might be viewed as impossible or uncomfortable threatens The Drift's desire for the status quo, for control, for survival. Master leaders rock the boat.

Remember, we human beings are driven by ego. We create our ego when we're children; we develop it in our early years and are driven by it throughout life. Anything that we perceive as a threat to the ego, to our interpretation of what is right, wrong, good, or bad makes us uncomfortable and skeptical.

The very nature of leadership is uncomfortable! The very nature of being a leader is to live an uncomfortable life. It's not just about getting out of the box. There is no box for a leader, which also means there is no obstacle that supersedes a leader's power including external obstacles like The Drift, the naysayers, the critics.

Felipe Avila, or Pipe, is a transformational trainer with Espacio Vital Global. Pipe is an incredibly passionate leader, parent, spouse, business owner, and contract attorney. "I left my business career to become a coach and trainer in transformation," he says. "This is about saving lives."

Pipe knows the truth of that statement, and about changing obstacles into opportunities in a visceral way. When he was 29, Pipe was kidnapped—one of the thousands kidnapped in Mexico every year.

"When I was kidnapped, I almost died," Pipe says. "In The Drift in Mexico, people are disconnected, living like robots. It's oppressive there. When someone puts their foot on you, you become a doormat. People lie down, say I don't care anymore, I just need to get by with my check. We have a victim culture."

Pipe does not choose to live in victim as many would in his circumstances. Instead, he's a committed maniac on a mission to shift The Drift. "I am living my vision to change the world. I don't want my kids—any kids—to live in a world with war, with fighting, with drugs. I want to make a better world for my kids. If it's going to be, it's up to me, and I will do everything in my power to transform it."

As long as ego is prevalent in our society, leaders face obstacles just by the air they breathe. Yet they don't stop. "My vision is bigger than any circumstances," Pipe says. "When I'm scared, I make fear my friend, and I take the risk."

MASTER LEADERS PLAN FOR OBSTACLES

When leaders declare a vision, part of the commitment to that vision is to create a plan of action, to create a strategy that bridges the gap to the completion of the vision. That strategy looks into the future—a year, two years, five years, ten years—to begin to bring the vision into the present. The plan is the who, what, where, when, and how of getting from where they are to where they want to be. In the process of developing that plan and strategy, obstacles will come up.

Seeing obstacles as opportunities is one of the first steps for any entrepreneur. In my experience, most entrepreneurs have the idea, the desire and the vision for their business. What most entrepreneurs do not have are the resources to make it happen. Another word for many entrepreneurs who fail is "wantrepreneur." They know what they want, but they've missed planning for financial obstacles.

Many of us have that friend or relative who's notorious for saying, "Hey, I've got a business idea I want to share with you." I have someone who's called me with no less than 25 business ideas in the last 20 years, and he always calls with incredible enthusiasm to share them — the concepts, the marketing, the expected results — everything except the resources, the money. He's the very definition of a wantrepreneur. His greatest obstacle is himself.

On the other side of the coin is an entrepreneur like James, who is 30 years old, financially successful and abundant. He sells exotic cars.

In the definition and expectation of The Drift, James shouldn't be successful. He doesn't have a formal education. He started a business he knew nothing about. He didn't know how to set up an organization, didn't know about licenses, LLC's, taxes, insurance or hiring.

But James had the vision. He had the desire, the commitment, the concept, the product, the service, and he put together a solid strategy plan. With his confidence in his own leadership, savvy people skills and a professional plan, he created the investors, the capital, to make the business work and become successful.

James had obstacles every step of the way. Right after I met him, his CEO resigned with two weeks' notice. Rather than being in breakdown or angry or feeling victimized by the news, James saw it as opportunity. He could very easily have chosen to be a victim to the circumstance of his CEO's decision. Instead, he was empowered by the opportunities and possibilities available with change, and he inspired me enough to tell his story. That's why he's successful.

LEADERS BELIEVE

I grew up in Boston, and I love the Boston Red Sox. They've given me one of my all-time favorite examples of leadership and turning obstacles into opportunities.

In 2004, the Red Sox (we) were down to the dreaded Yankees, three games to zero in game four of the American League Championship Series, it was the best of seven. We were down four runs to three in the bottom of the ninth inning and three outs away from being knocked out of the playoffs and swept by the Yankees, again.

Mariano Rivera was pitching; he is the best closing pitcher in the history of baseball. All he needed to do was get three outs.

Now, the Red Sox had a team meeting earlier in the day, and all the players agreed: "We're down, but we're not out. All we need is one."

Red Sox iconic first baseman Kevin Millar started telling his fellow players to "Cowboy Up," and that motto permeated the energy of the team. Kevin Millar inspired and instilled confidence in his team despite the odds against them. When they faced the obstacle of three games to zero in a best of seven series and were down by one run in the bottom of the ninth AND the best and greatest closer in the history of baseball was pitching, the odds of us winning that game were about 99 to 1 against. I mean, forget the Series.

Naturally, the first guy up was Kevin Millar. He drew a walk to lead off the bottom of the ninth and was immediately replaced by pinch-runner Dave Roberts who stole second base. Bill Mueller got a base hit and drove him in. The game was tied in the bottom of the ninth.

We won the game in extra innings with a walk-off home run by Big Papi, David Ortiz. After the game, Kevin Millar was in the news saying, "I told you. Don't let us win one! Don't let us win one!" He was still out there inspiring his team, turning obstacles into opportunities.

After that, the Red Sox clicked and won the next three games. No team in the history of baseball had ever won a playoff series down three games to zero.

The team came back and won the series four games to three and went on to the World Series and won four to zero. The Red Sox steamrolled their way into winning the championship. It was the first time the Red Sox had won a World Series in 86 years!

My point is, there's always another way. The Sox—as they declared as a team—were down but not out. Most people had given up on them. Kevin Millar didn't give up. His teammates didn't give up. I never gave up. I watched every minute of that game, every minute of the series. I believed in that team in the face of no historical evidence to do so.

Here's the power of vision and an example of a point I made at the beginning of this distinction: When a leader declares a vision to cause or create something, to reach into the future to bring that vision into the present, they declare eventual results consistent with the vision.

On my 40th birthday that year, a month and a half before the world series, my family and friends got me a cake with the Boston Red Sox logo and the words "World Series Champions 2004." Everyone knew I was 100 percent enrolled in the vision of the Red Sox (reversing the curse of the Bambino) winning for the first time in 86 years because I shouted it from the top of my lungs of every town and city I visited in 2004 and to anyone who would listen. I didn't care what they thought of me nor did I care about the overwhelming evidence that it's not possible. The obstacles were clearly perception and interpretation.

What were the obstacles in the way of my vision for the Red Sox and their eventual results? Eighty-six years of failure and crushing game-seven losses in other World Series opportunities.

Master leaders and visionaries accept and expect obstacles and turn them into opportunities. I declared out loud to everybody I knew that the Red Sox would win the series, and we weren't even in the playoffs yet. Had they not won, I would have gotten so much grief from my students, my clients, my friends! They would have loved to get my goat, to see me be wrong in my declaration because, in The Drift, we often take pleasure when others fail.

But I was courageous and visionary and vulnerable and willing to put my heart on the line. That's how much I believed in my team. Did I win the game for them? Of course not. I took an out-loud committed stand against all the odds to declare that the Red Sox would win the World Series. I didn't keep it to myself. I shouted it from the rooftops.

And you can do the same, in your vision for your family, your future spouse, your business, your health, your team. Stand in your vision with rigorous acceptance. Declare it out loud. Embrace it. Work with it. Believe in it. Commit to it. Get involved in it.

Figure out how to build your vision. How to create it, design it, redesign it, invent it. Craft your plan, your strategy, and take action. Don't stop until you make it happen, regardless of what challenges come up, or what obstacles appear. Period.

By the way, since I started writing this book in early 2017, I declared—before the season began—that the Red Sox would win the 2018 World Series. Guess what? A lot of my friends thought I was crazy and delusional, and I took a bunch of flak from the Drift. On October 28th, 2018, the Red Sox won their 4th World Series Championship in the last 15 years. Ironically, since 2004. Make room for number 5…

**OBSTACLES:
HURDLES ARE OPPORTUNITIES**

Name three to five internal and external obstacles that are prohibiting you from creating your vision?

_____

_____

_____

_____

_____

_____

_____

_____

_____

_____

If you change your perception from obstacle to opportunity, what's possible for you?

_____

_____

_____

_____

_____

_____

_____

_____

DISTINCTION 9 – OBSTACLES

Using foresight, what are the key obstacles you see right now and in the future as you pursue your vision?

_____

_____

_____

_____

_____

_____

_____

_____

_____

_____

What are the declarations and beliefs you stand for with rigorous acceptance?

_____

_____

_____

_____

_____

_____

_____

_____

_____

_____

DISTINCTION 10

WISDOM: APPLYING LESSONS LEARNED

Wisdom: the quality or state of being wise; knowledge of what is true or right coupled with just judgment as to action; sagacity, discernment, or insight.

Master leader's definition: the profound awareness to make choices and decisions in the now, while simultaneously learning from previous experience. Understanding the law of cause and effect.

"Being a wise thinker means I go beyond what is obvious. I consider, I pay attention, and I move towards a wise decision. Seeing all of the possibilities is what is beautiful to me about the work of transformation and leadership." – Elizabeth Lara (Ely) Caputo, Co-Founder and CEO of 4D Associates International

---

Master leaders are wise thinkers. Wisdom comes from experience, from being able to distinguish between what works and what doesn't work and apply the lessons learned from both without attaching judgment to either. A wise

149

leader knows how to be neutral to what goes on around him or her and objectively see the value in what's taking place no matter how it appears. True leaders learn from mistakes as well as successes, knowing both are equally important in the process of discovery and growth.

Master leaders understand that the most successful people in the world experience failure more often than they experience success, but they don't relate to failure in the same way that most do. To leaders, failure is an opportunity to learn, just as succeeding is an opportunity to learn. It is this learning that makes leaders wise, and it is this wisdom that reveals the true leaders taking a stand in The Drift.

WISDOM AT 35,000 FEET

When we apply mastery of leadership and the previous distinctions to a conversation about wisdom and transformation, wise thinkers emerge as those who understand and can apply the nuance of this statement: I am using my thoughts. I am not being used by my thoughts.

Wise thinkers use their thoughts and their ability to formulate ideas, concepts, and possibilities, seeing beyond what's in front of them and in a real sense, what I like to call seeing from a 35,000-foot view.

Wise thinkers operate from that perspective. With a 35,000-foot approach to life, how far can you see? It looks like infinity, like endless possibility. To a master leader, wisdom is the ability to use a broad perspective to bridge the gap between the concept of your vision and the manifestation of it. It is seeing clearly how to get from where you are and where you want to be as well as the space between your declared and desired results.

When we're in the early stages of creating something new, we often get tunnel vision rather than having far-reaching perspective.

We get stuck on one thought, one concept, one idea, one strategy. It's possible to find value in that, especially when that narrowed view is evidence of rigor and focus, and is keeping you in your vision, closing any backdoors and locking yourself into commitment. Having no backup plan sometimes works, specifically for "dreamers" who typically don't complete or follow through.

But tunnel vision also can put you on a railroad track that goes in only one direction or moves only in a straight line. It narrows your perspective, and, if that's how you consistently approach your vision, your business, your sales strategy, your relationships—the things that truly matter to you—you will miss out on infinite possibilities.

That's the value of taking a 35,000-foot view, where you can clearly see the horizon and a world of possibility, limitless ways and strategies to accomplish your vision.

WISDOM IS IN THE LEARNING

What makes any venture or vision thrive—not just survive—is the application of ongoing wisdom.

Take any successful company on the day of a new product launch. The marketing and advertising and sales teams are on it, getting it out there and doing their jobs. It's a full court press, all hands on deck.

What's the research and development team doing after all their hard work? Basking in their own glow? Maybe for a day or two, but, as we discussed in Distinction 9, almost instantaneously, the R&D team is more interested in what's missing in that product than what's working with it.

The focus shifts to making it better, improving it, and taking what doesn't work and solving and resolving those issues. That's what makes thriving organizations like Apple, Amazon, and

Google propel into the never-ending expansion of the vision. They stay true to the application of real learning.

Wisdom is in the learning. That's when leaders dissect what worked and what didn't work. They use the feedback, roll up their sleeves and ask valuable curious questions. Who benefits from this product? Who are we reaching and who are we missing in our marketing strategy? How are our systems functioning to support the launch? What are our blind spots? What's missing that we are committed to fixing so that the next product launch has a higher level of success? What's working in the leadership? What's not working in the leadership?

And then leaders get back into the game of declaring what's next—over and over again. One of the things I love about the work of transformation is that no matter what breakthrough you have, no matter how effective you are at what you're creating, there's always a 'what's next' available to you, your people and your organization.

My friend, colleague, and former student Shanda Sumpter has by any standards created incredible success and abundance in both her business and professional life. Shanda is the founder and queen visionary of the multi-million-dollar HeartCore Business, an entrepreneurial coaching company. She's also a speaker, trainer, bestselling author, wife, and mom.

If Shanda wanted to, she could quit right now. She's created magic and abundance. She could walk away from her company and build sandcastles with her family at their ocean-front home. Instead, Shanda's a master leader dedicated to transforming the world.

Shanda's at 35,000 feet, present and driven by future-focused vision. And she's wise.

"I just realized the other day that I'm almost halfway through my life. I was sitting up on my rooftop deck thinking that I'm 43 years old and the average woman lives to 87. I intend to live far past that, but if I was to fall into the average category, then I'm almost halfway done my life. And I was asking myself what do I want the next half to look like?" Shanda says.

"And really what the answer came down to is how can I be more generous? How can I be a more generous mother? How can I give more to my son? How can I give more to my marriage? What would my marriage look like if I gave more to it? How far can I grow this company? How big can I get it? How many people can I transform and help? But then at the bottom of all of that is the realization that what it all really comes down to is I just want to know that my life mattered."

Undoubtedly that is the case; however, Shanda, like all master leaders, understands that it is her ability to focus out, to create win/wins for all that reaps extraordinary results.

WISDOM IS NEUTRAL

Wisdom is standing in the middle of the fire, the fire of life, the fire of a vision, the fire of a commitment, the fire of the marriage and children, the fire of something that matters. And when standing in the fire is challenging, or stressful or uncomfortable or fearful, master leaders remain neutral and have access to the power of using the mind to create infinite possibilities. They do not indulge in victim conversations. The moment leaders choose victim they lose all power and access to wisdom.

Master leaders have incredible wisdom. They look at every situation from the standpoint of who do I need to be and what do I need to do in order to cause what I'm committed to causing?

They don't look at challenging situations or circumstances through the filters of emotion or impressing others. They don't worry about looking good or being right.

I'm not saying leaders aren't emotional. Emotion fuels passion and results and even wisdom. Leaders understand that it's as important to celebrate their wins, to experience the joy and exuberance of a job well done as it is to experience the feelings and disappointments in the losses, the things that don't work. Clearing the space is healthy emotionally, mentally and physically. Clearing the space allows the opportunity for lessons and wisdom.

But at some point—and the harder they practice, the faster it happens—master leaders step out of the feelings, emotions, judgments, and opinions of the circumstance and get to the application of the lessons learned—in action with a sense of urgency—because they understand what's at stake.

In other words, they don't waste time or energy falling back into a survival context. They're aware, of course, that they have a survival context, they're aware that they have survival conversations, that they have ego conversations and limiting beliefs, but they don't let those ego conversations become more important than their choices, actions, and results.

Master leaders don't react. They respond. The idea of mastery of leadership is cause-cause, not cause and effect. There's a quote attributed to Gandhi that says, "an eye for an eye makes the whole world blind." That's an incredibly wise concept, particularly in the context of master leadership. It's human nature to react to something. If somebody hits you, it's human nature to want to lash out, to fight back or hit back.

In The Drift, bullying creates bullies. In my trainings, I ask the students to raise their hands if they've ever been bullied. Consistently, 90 percent raise their hands. That means physical bullying, mental bullying, emotional bullying, and nowadays with social media and digital photos, it often means sexual bullying.

Many of those that raise their hands acknowledge that they too have been bullies to others. The bullies in our world are often bullied themselves first.

Through wisdom, we have the power to use our minds to formulate appropriate responses personally and professionally without lowering ourselves into a survival battle and fight between our egos and the world around us.

WISDOM LEARNS FROM ITS MISTAKES

How do we apply wisdom in the context of neutrality vs. victim and reaction? By going back to the core of where something comes from and resolving it at the source.

How do you fight fire? Not with fire. The fire department doesn't show up with fire. The fire department shows up with water.

How do you resolve a breakdown in a relationship when both of you are right? All it takes is one of you to throw in the towel, show humility, and acknowledge the breakdown, to apologize and be responsible. It only takes one to be in ownership and have the wisdom to realize that as a couple this breakdown is not the sum total of their relationship or life together.

Master leaders have access to wisdom. Victims have access to pain, suffering, sarcasm, empty promises, stories, excuses, justifications, mediocrity. People in victim mentality can't access wisdom. They can't learn from their mistakes. They aren't responsible for their errors or what created them in the first place.

We've all seen victim in action, especially when it comes to relationships. You've likely had an experience similar to this: You're out with friends, and you're sharing stories about your love life, about your vision for your next relationship. The conversation goes south when someone else starts talking about how bad their marriage is; it's awful and boring, and that's just the way it is, and it's never going to get better. Perhaps you and your friends start to counsel that person, coach that person, maybe give that person feedback and or advice, helpful hints, ideas, and positive reinforcement.

But they can't hear you. They're stuck in the belief (and a relationship) defined by the belief that nothing's going to change, and it doesn't matter what you say. Is that applying wisdom to their life? Is that person responsible? Is that person learning from mistakes?

Or consider businesses that offer products or services and receive feedback or information that something isn't working, yet they do nothing to change it. A classic example is the Ford Pinto, a small car built in the 1970s with a known-issue: in rear-end crashes the fuel tank failed and often caught fire. *Popular Mechanics* called it "possibly the best example of what happens when poor engineering meets corporate negligence."

That corporate negligence went on for years. People died. Ford's leadership at the time pushed the car into production, with full awareness of its dangers, to compete with emerging competition from Japanese automakers. Ironically the Japanese market grew, and Ford still sports a black eye for their decision to put profit over people and their safety.

Wisdom is learning from your mistakes, learning from your failures, learning from your breakdowns. Wisdom is also learning from success, from what's working. Wisdom is applying those lessons to your next level, your next declaration, your next company, your next relationship.

If research and design strategies are not in place in your vision, whether it's personal or professional, then the vision doesn't have life. Vision must have an on-going "what's next?" An on-going, "So what, now what?"

Once you've launched whatever it is you're launching with your vision, your job as a master leader is to get back into research, get back into the lab, come up with something new, something cutting edge, that wasn't going to be created anyway.

WISDOM BEYOND YEARS

Wisdom comes from your experience of being in the process, from your ability to learn from any and all of the commitments in your life on an ongoing basis. It has to do with contribution; it has to do with giving, it has to do with seeing a possibility where one doesn't exist. It has to do with changing direction, changing course when the path you're on isn't working. It comes from the realization that "I have met the enemy and it is I." It comes from owning your responsibility, owning your accountability.

Wisdom comes from getting away from being right and realizing that your marriage is more important—that your lover or your husband or wife or partner—is more important than your need to be right about a particular issue. Wisdom comes from interrupting patterns and not repeating the past. Wisdom comes from changing behaviors and living the change.

Wisdom doesn't have anything to do with age. In a lot of older people, cynicism passes for wisdom. They respond to life from a place of knowing it all, as in, "I know because I was there. I know because of what happened in the past." But often what they have to contribute is cynicism, judgment or pontification about how things used to be, or should be now. Everything was better back in the day. That's not wisdom. That's arrogance.

I think children are wise. When my stepson Conner was about eight years old, he said to his mom, "Hey, Mom. Let me get this straight. You carried me in your stomach for nine months?" Hillary said yes. "And then you gave birth to me?" Hillary said yes. And Conner, fresh from science class at school, thinking in practical application and putting two and two together the way kids do, asked, "Doesn't that make you a mad scientist?" Not only is that adorable, but it's also wise thinking.

The wisdom of kids can sometimes make an impact where adults can't. White House Press Secretary Sarah Huckabee Sanders often gives non-answer answers to questions from the media about virtually every controversial topic, including school shootings and gun control. But when 13-year-old Benie Choucroun, a reporter from *TIME for Kids*, asked her the same type of question, she visibly choked up, on camera.

"One thing that affects my and other students' mental health is the worry about the fact that we or our friends could get shot at school," Benie said. Specifically, can you tell me what the Administration has done and will do to prevent these senseless tragedies?"

Huckabee-Sanders got vulnerable, which she doesn't normally do, and responded authentically and beautifully. "I think that as a kid and certainly as a parent there is nothing that could be more terrifying for a kid to go to school and not feel safe," she said, with raw emotion in her voice.

Think about how often children step into the middle of a conflict with parents and say, "can't we just love each other or please stop fighting." Kids often make requests that come from unadulterated wisdom.

Here's another example from the Strasner family.

Yesterday I was talking to Haley, my stepdaughter. She didn't want to study for her final. We were sitting on the couch, and I said, "You know what, babe? If I only did the things I want to do and not the things that are important for me to do, I would almost never get off this couch. And do you see this remote that's in my hand right now? You would have to pry it from my fingers.

"Because what I want to do is nothing. What I want to do is eat pizza. What I want to do is play golf. What I want to do (and I didn't say this to her, but I was thinking it) is bond with my wife."

I told Haley there are plenty of things I want to do, but there are also things that are important, like the work I do. People count on me to make a difference in their lives. They count on me to deliver coaching that will cause them or evoke in them the ability to see something that they've never seen before, to connect with the vision that they have never imagined, and then take action on it to create a life worth living.

As a result of the work I do, I get paid, and I get invited to come back. And through that compensation you get to go to cheerleading and cheerleading camp, you get to have friends over and order Mexican food and have pool parties in the pool we can afford to have cleaned so that you can swim in it.

I said, "Haley, the difference between you and me is that I don't let what I want and how I feel dictate my actions."

And she said what every teenager would say, which is "Yeah, but I'm not an adult yet." I said, "That's true. But one day you will be an adult, and you will want to be prepared. You will want to be confident in your ability to create what you want in your life and be compensated for it. That doesn't happen by magic or by sitting on the couch.

"What it requires is that you study for your finals and put the effort in. When you commit yourself to doing as well as you can, vs. just getting by, what message does that give to your mom? How does it impact mom? Do you think it makes her happy?"

The answer was yes, of course. I said, "Okay then when you say, 'Hey Mom, when we go to Florida can I bring a friend,' do you think mom is going to more likely or less likely to say yes?"

Because the point is, everything is cause/cause. You show up a certain way, act a certain way, you create a certain result. You generate possibilities for yourself.

I didn't plan to have that conversation with her. It came out of listening to her and what she was saying. I applied real-time wisdom to her possibilities so that she could engage it and then see it. A few minutes later she left to go upstairs to study.

I learned from my parents what worked and didn't work. I realize that there are many ways to inspire somebody and the way that I inspired Haley is different than the approach I would use with her brother. Just as master communication requires various pitches, the same is true for wisdom.

I think of wisdom as the ability to apply the incredible genius that is our minds and use it to create magic and possibilities in life. Wisdom is proactive, not passive, which reminds me of a quote from a wise child who has grown into an adult example for us all.

"If one man can destroy everything, why can't one girl change it?" — Malala Yousafzai

WISDOM:
APPLYING LESSONS LEARNED

For me, wisdom is…

_____
_____
_____
_____
_____
_____
_____
_____
_____
_____

How can you apply wisdom to your life? Where is wisdom lacking?

_____
_____
_____
_____
_____
_____
_____
_____
_____

If you're creating cause-cause in your relationships, what difference will it make?

_____

_____

_____

_____

_____

_____

_____

_____

_____

_____

_____

_____

What does your vision and life look like from 35,000 feet?

_____

_____

_____

_____

_____

_____

_____

_____

_____

_____

_____

DISTINCTION 11

CHARACTER: UNDENIABLE INTEGRITY AND GRACE

Character: the mental and moral qualities distinctive to an individual.
Master leader's definition: the behavior, thoughts, and actions of the leader are predictably and unmistakably admired, respected, and revered.

Master leadership is not so much about doing anything; it's about being. It's about being a master leader, being an example of what's possible with everybody that you come in contact with, no matter what you're doing.
– Myrna Gonzalez, transformational trainer and coach

Master leaders have incredible strength of character. Character is the undeniable way of being that causes people to follow someone and not know why, to look up to someone and want to emulate them for no specific reason. Leaders have such character. When they walk into a room, they somehow stand out without saying anything. They "show up" as significant because of the way they carry themselves, yet they never need to draw attention to themselves.

Master leaders embody specific characteristics. They are compassionate, sensitive, understanding, and forgiving. They are powerful, energetic, courageous, and joyous. They are honest and authentic with themselves and others while being committed to the truth. They look for the positive in all situations without losing their grasp on reality. Leaders persevere, never selling out or giving up on their vision, commitments, or values while always accepting with humility the difficulties that life offers up. There is an easy and peaceful way about them, a balance that is natural. Leaders who lead with character redefine what it means to be alive.

LEADERS WITH CHARACTER REDEFINE WHAT IT MEANS TO BE ALIVE

Master leaders redefine what it means to be alive because true leaders will not tolerate or settle for mediocrity. I think most people in The Drift are satisfied with a life that is based on some form of survival or reasonable fulfillment in some capacity. Their reasoning might sound like this, "I have a job, I make money, and I can pay my bills. It's not the job I went to college for; it's not what I studied. It's not the best job I can have. It's not the most rewarding job or opportunity I have had, but it is a reasonable job. It's considered a good job by society." Does that sound familiar?

I think that most people who are in a relationship—especially in The Drift—would classify their relationship as "good," or "fine," or "okay." They might use terms like "the wife" to describe their spouse. I had someone in a training the other day who called his girlfriend "my woman," and he said it in a way of being that was extremely controlling. It wasn't an acknowledgment of her. It was almost as if there was a caveman in the room who was dragging his lefthanded knuckles on the ground and his girlfriend by the hair behind him with his other hand.

Leaders are not okay with okay. Leaders do not settle for fine. Or "could be better/could be worse." Or "not bad." Or "my woman."

STRENGTH OF CHARACTER LIVES IN THE PRESENT

Many people in The Drift are living a life that includes some version of fueling themselves by sucking the fumes of a past accomplishment or experience, running down the gas in the tank, and not realizing they're losing fuel.

Leaders with strength of character don't operate that way. Leaders are people who carve out and create the future. Leaders are people that declare the future. Leaders are people that expect the highest version of themselves and the highest version of what's possible for themselves. Leaders don't play the game of life just to play or play not to lose. Leaders play the game of life to win, for everyone in the family, in the company, in the world.

Of course, winning is subjective in a lot of areas and a lot of ways, so let's look at the context of mastery of leadership and "winning" in a relationship.

Is the pinnacle of your relationship—its defining and most memorable moment—yesterday, last week, last month, last year, your honeymoon, Valentine's Day four years ago? If something in the past was the pinnacle of the relationship and you're using that as the way to fuel your connection currently, then eventually your relationship is going to run out of gas. Joy is not in the past. Passion is not in the past. When it comes to a relationship, love and passion are experiences and ways of being that are created in the present, in the moment.

If you are in a relationship and you are not actively engaged in making it the way you want it to be today, in the moment, you're not creating the magic that's available to you.

If somebody asks you to rate your relationship on a scale of zero to ten, and you rate it a seven, the next question to yourself should be, "was it ever a ten?" If it was, but it's currently a seven, what does that mean? It means the air is leaking slowly out of the balloon. It means the gas is leaking from the tank of your relationship. It means that you're not creating, recreating, or generating a breakthrough to redesign how you're showing up in that relationship.

Maybe there is an issue or breakdown in the relationship that one or both of you is determined to be right about. And being right about the breakdown has become more important than creating a "ten" relationship. This situation creates a choice moment of prime awareness.

In realizing that, a master leader with strength of character will begin moving the seven back to a ten, to bring back joy and passion to the present and stop resting on the laurels of the past. To begin to "win" at the relationship, which might also include creating the opening for honest, straight talk about the issue or breakdown with the intention of clearing it and working past it, to forgive and start anew.

I think a lot of people are nostalgic about their lives, living in the past and attached to the accomplishments or experiences that make them most proud. Nostalgia can bring a certain sense of joy or empowerment, but it does not offer the power that's born in the present. Nostalgia about something in the past doesn't bring the same kind of juice to life as accomplishing in the now brings. And over time, it dissipates. It doesn't regenerate; it doesn't rejuvenate. There's no sense of newness.

I'm a prime example. I love the game of golf, and I've spent 37 years sucking every bit of juice out of the experience of getting my first hole in one, which happened when I was 17 years old. At the time, I expected I would have many more hole-in-ones. I thought, "I'm only 17, and I've only been playing for three years. I'll probably get 20 or 25 more of these in my life."

And here I am at 54, still looking for my second hole in one. Let me tell you, the nostalgia of that experience has lost its juice! For 37 years, I've been committed to getting another hole in one, and I have not achieved that vision. So now when I talk about it (which I rarely do), more than anything it brings up judgment and frustration and disappointment for me. A feeling of "womp-womp" – it's the "you lose" sound from a game show.

How is it possible that I have not attained this vision? I'm a very good golfer, and no one could possibly miss a hole-in-one more often than I have. I've hit the pin and missed. I've left the ball literally hanging on the edge of the hole. I've bounced it out and rolled it over the hole.

After I hit that first hole in one when I was 17, I would talk about it to anyone who asked me. And it would bring me nostalgic joy and excitement along with eager anticipation and expectation that the next one was right around the corner.

Now, when I'm unconscious about it, the cynical voice in my head says, "You haven't had a hole in one in 37 years. You're not going to get one now." And then my other voice, the conscious leader, says, "Okay, it's a new moment, a new possibility. Focus your mind, clear your vision, clear your intention. What and how are you going to hit it? You can knock this ball in! Focus, be present, and make the shot."

That's 37 years of working on focus, living in the moment, and interrupting my negative self-talk. Master leaders persevere, never selling out or giving up on their vision, commitments, or values while always accepting with humility the difficulties that life (and golf) offer up.

STRENGTH OF CHARACTER IS A WAY OF BEING

Incredible strength of character is a way of being, a way of being in relationship with ourselves. The way we relate to ourselves is the context that creates our external relationships with the outside world—our husbands, wives, lovers, colleagues, business partners, children. Leaders with incredible strength of character embody the ways of being that are attractive, admired, respected, wanted, and revered by the outside world.

The outside world recognizes strength of character when it walks into a room. Some people have that certain je ne sais quoi, that unexplainable something. They walk into a room, and they're somehow taller than everybody in the space; they're powerful, charismatic, glowing. It's almost as if they operate from a spa-like experience inside their body. They exude grace, ease, and confidence, even when they are in pressure-packed situations.

Other people see in them the calm in the storm, the certainty of what's possible, the impeccable integrity that they espouse. You see it in all types of people: grandmothers, grandfathers, teachers. You can see it in some leaders. You can see it in certain athletes like LeBron James. As a life-long Celtics fan, I hesitate to use him as an example because I am not a fan of the Cleveland Cavaliers. And now, even worse, he's with the Los Angeles Lakers! However, Lebron James is a great example of incredible strength of character because there is overwhelming evidence that he walks the talk in his basketball playing, life, relationship and in the community.

He's still married to his high school sweetheart. How many athletes are still married to their high school sweetheart after 15 years and millions of dollars? No one questions his integrity. There's no talk of him with other women. There's no drama with him and his business relationships. He has a calmness about him that attracts people to his larger-than-life ways of being. He's a beacon of possibility. James exudes an incredible strength of character that makes people want to follow him. He was the leader of the Cavs; they believed in him and rose to his level of excellence. Unfortunately, I'm sure he'll create those same results with the Lakers.

John F. Kennedy had a similar way of being. My dad saw him speak at his high school; when he saw him from the other side of the street, he said there was a glow about him and a way of being that inspired every person there. JFK created a buzz, and it lit people up—to vote for him, to be like him, to be part of his vision. His vision was large, but it was his way of being that my dad remembered the most. He doesn't remember the speech, but he remembers how he felt when he saw Kennedy.

He had an undeniable presence.

However, I would not say JFK had incredible strength of character at the master leader level. Leaders with impeccable character are also defined by their actions and behaviors. JFK had some character challenges, but his vision and achievements are legendary. He was the first Roman Catholic to be elected to the presidency and the change he shaped in the United States and the world in less than three years in office is irrefutable.

Nelson Mandela had that way of being. Barack Obama has it. In terms of strength of character, Obama is closer to mastery. He walks the talk. He brought to the presidency and his personal life a deep level of dignity, intellect, empathy, and grace. During his eight years in office, the government had minimal scandals, seemingly the least amount of any other president in modern times. Considering that his opponents were relentlessly committed to taking him down as a President and person, no evidence has emerged that he's ever been anything but faithful to his wife and committed to his children.

In my position as a trainer and leader, people constantly approach me with offers and opportunities. I true up my choices, decisions, and actions through my vision and values. This results in consistency of not only the message but also the messenger.

STRENGTH OF CHARACTER PERSEVERES

Having incredible and impeccable strength of character isn't just a way of being. It's also acting with responsibility and integrity and aligning oneself with walking the talk of master leadership. Being out of integrity or disingenuous is not an option to a master leader.

Master leaders are human beings that have learned to be self-cleaning ovens. They not only stand for others but also pay attention to their own needs. Master leaders are aware and present to solving experiences or situations that create conflict, without compounding the breakdown. This is where character comes in.

When you are impeccable and rigorous with your word, you are developing your own context of character. We have a choice in all situations. Do you react, or do you respond? Master leaders respond. Do you vent with the purpose of being right or do you vent to let something go? You vent to let something go because a master leader isn't attached to being right.

What is the difference between going out to have a couple of drinks and going out to get drunk? Or the difference between taking an Uber and driving under the influence? Or the difference between paying your taxes and cheating by hiding your money? It's simple, character.

If you have strength of character, you are responsible and proactive. You think in the future, anticipate your choices and possibilities and you act on those choices that serve you and the world in highest possibility. You don't cut corners, and you don't manipulate situations or people.

People who have incredible and impeccable strength of character are honest and trustworthy. Master leaders don't sugar-coat; they don't edit, don't calculate. They might communicate honesty in different forms so that it's empowering or can be heard by the listener, but they don't lie or manipulate the context of their communication for their audience. Master leaders don't say to their brother, "I love you, and you're amazing" and then say to their sister, "Our brother's an asshole and I can't stand him."

People who have incredible strength of character do not gossip. The Drift is full of gossip. Relationships are gossipy. The office is gossipy. What do you think people talk about most of the time at work when they're not focusing on their job? They're talking about the people at work. They're talking about the boss, and they're talking about the people they don't like.

It seems to me that our current president not only enjoys fame and celebrity, but also the gossip that comes with it. I used to think The National Enquirer was the champion of generating gossip in our society, but it now has strong competition from President Trump. The terms he uses, such as "some people are saying," or "many people are saying," or "everyone is saying," are the language of gossip.

Character changes the gossip conversation. It asks, "Is what I'm going to say moving the vision forward? Does what I'm going to say add value? People who have incredible strength of character focus on adding value in a relationship, in business, in a company, everywhere they can.

The focus is on adding value, empowering that person or that situation to go to a higher level of effectiveness, a higher level of success, a higher level of love, a higher level of connection.

People who have incredible strength and character are givers. They're generous with their time, attitudes, thoughts, and interpretations. They're operating from authenticity.

People who have incredible strength and character are in a clean space. They're enrolled in the vision, and the vision comes through the door before they do.

Lately, Barack Obama has been saying he might have been president 20 years too early. I believe his strength of character and vision got him elected because he was certainly very young to be president. He had little leadership or business management experience. He inherited tremendous breakdowns in his presidency. The United States needed a leader that would steady the ship.

Maybe the country wasn't ready for him, but he certainly accomplished many aspects of his mission. You can argue with his policies and results, but it's hard to argue that the ship needed a steadfast, consistent leader, someone with character.

Barack Obama demonstrated an unwavering sense of grace under extreme pressure. He possessed a powerful strength in standing up to extraordinary challenges without selling out his dignity or integrity in the process.

Master leaders with incredible strength of character live their word. When they say they're going to do something, it's a done deal. You can take it to the bank. That doesn't happen in The Drift where character erodes every day into distrust, skepticism, and cynicism, where there's an unprecedented lack of integrity and honor regarding our word.

The Drift is loudly skeptical; it doesn't trust anyone or anything without proof. Master leaders in the work of transformation shift that experience. We make the distinction between who someone is and how they behave. For example, I trust people until they give me a reason not to trust them. Can you imagine a world where we trust each other unconditionally? It would knock down the walls of our comfort zones and light up possibility for everyone.

My son Nick will tell you this about me: "I can predict what my dad will do or how he will respond in almost any situation." Why? Well, he might say it's because I'm boring and predictable and for sure that may be part of it. But I also believe he will say it's because I'm consistent and steadfast in how I show up for him. He'd say, "I

DISTINCTION 11 – CHARACTER

know I can count on him for his unconditional love and support, always."

I'm not perfect (not even close), but I am rigorous in how I show up for my wife and children. They get my 100 percent best all the time.

STRENGTH OF CHARACTER CONTRIBUTES

You, if you choose, can become a Master Leader and shift The Drift through embodying the principles of master leadership. The world is screaming for master leaders; there's no time and no need to wait for the next Jackie Robinson or Oprah or Malala to emerge.

Master leaders can and do make a difference in The Drift in a myriad of ways—from the PTA, local politics, the principal's office, or the kitchen. Master leaders know they don't require a job title or permission to lead. They use vision and the distinctions to take committed action in all aspects of our society, to stand up for what's possible.

You may recall wise thinker Shanda Sumpter from the chapter on Distinction 10. Shanda's company, Heartcore Business, provides programs built to generate business for entrepreneurs while using their distinct individual gifts.

"My experience is that everybody wants to make money, and make a difference," Shanda says. "But at the end of the day, most people don't take responsibility for making a difference unless they're getting paid. I'm crazy enough to actually think that I can change the world, and I want more people to believe that about themselves.

"Every single one of us has a piece of the puzzle, we all have something really important to contribute. I think people don't contribute as much as they think they do, because they don't get that they matter. They spend their lives working on themselves, not understanding that everything they're working on in themselves will be fixed if they contribute. Everything they don't like about themselves, every procrastination, every self-doubt, every worry about how they look, is fixed when people operate in contribution. But until they learn to do that, and get that they matter, they'll never be able to transform The Drift."

Master leaders contribute their gifts to the world through vision and empowerment, love and responsibility, integrity and character. You can stand for the future for your children, your family, your business, and your community using the 12 Distinctions of Master Leaders to evoke inspiration and contribution in others.

You can be the leader that walks into a room with an undeniable way of being that causes people to follow. You can redefine to the world what it means to be alive.

CHARACTER: UNDENIABLE INTEGRITY AND GRACE

Do you possess character, or do you show up as a character?

_____
_____
_____
_____
_____
_____
_____
_____
_____
_____

Be honest with yourself, are you a giver or a taker? Generous or stingy?

_____
_____
_____
_____
_____
_____
_____
_____
_____
_____

Are you genuinely proud of who you are? Why or why not?

_____

_____

_____

_____

_____

_____

_____

_____

_____

_____

Are you liked, admired, and respected by people other than your family?

_____

_____

_____

_____

_____

_____

_____

_____

_____

_____

DISTINCTION 12

CREATING LEADERS: IGNITING THE INTERNAL FLAME

Ignite: to catch fire or cause to catch fire.
Master Leader's definition: to inspire, evoke, and awaken the dormant vision in another, to light the spark.

> Leaders develop leadership in others. That's what a true leader does. Once you become a leader, transform yourself, and let go of your past, your job is to develop and shape other leaders. This is my life purpose. –Nacho Pérez Deco, co-founder, coach & trainer, Energía Positiva

Master leaders cause leadership in others. This is not only an art form but also the truest test of leadership. A leader knows that he or she has mastered something when they are able to cause someone else to master it as well. Leaders realize that no one achieves their vision alone.

Leadership implies other people, community. It involves building on the inherent strength in numbers and causing each individual to align with a common purpose. Leaders are natural team builders who maximize human potential. They recognize the abilities that people don't see in themselves and empower them to develop those abilities through intention and practice. Leaders develop extraordinary and winning teams.

Master leaders understand that teamwork is not simply about everyone doing their part. A team is not an assembly line that stops when one piece breaks down, but rather an organized structure of individuals who are each working in harmony towards a common goal. Leaders understand that the whole is greater than the sum of its parts, and each part is a necessary component toward success. They lead by example and in doing so teach others to lead.

THE CENTER OF INTENTION

Let's begin this last chapter with the context of where this distinction comes from. It's the idea that transformation doesn't have a life of its own. Transformation—and the possibility of creating a transformed life, family, relationship, company, or world--cannot happen unless there is leadership on all levels, from top to bottom.

Creating leadership in others is the idea of creating partners who stand alongside the leader as source, as if they thought of the vision on their own. When I create leadership in another person, I'm not giving them myself; I'm recreating myself in them. I'm recreating my vision in them, or the concept of the idea in them, in such a way that they then take it and create and recreate it in their own voice, in their own actions, and in the results that they produce as a consequence. Cause-cause.

Many years ago, when I was at the beginning of my career in the work of transformation, I had a coach and mentor named Jim Cook. I watched him lead, facilitate and coach, as well as listening intently to everything he said. Jim was 20 years older and a veteran trainer in this work. I respected him and held him high. He was married, had children, and was faithful and responsible, truly a man of character.

Jim and I were having dinner one night, and I was soaking him in, listening to him share his experience in transformation and what this work meant to him, why he did it, and what it was like to be a trainer. At some point, I asked him to give me feedback on his experience of me because I was committed to being a trainer and committed to becoming—like him—a master in this work.

He looked at me and said, "Michael Strasner, you are the best at what you do in the entire company. You are the number one enroller in your sales position. You are amazing with your love for people, your passion, your commitment, your willingness to do whatever it takes."

Jim went on and on in his five-minute acknowledgment of me. I was almost levitating at the table, hearing this person that I held in such esteem say such amazing things about me. And, of course, I was fully empowered and lit up!

And then he stopped and asked, "Now. Are you ready to have your next level of breakthrough?" And I told him yes, absolutely, 100 percent, because I was empowered and full and rich and excited about what he'd said to me. I was so wide open!

Jim said, "Michael, you are a star, a superstar with a bright future, but you are not a star maker. If you want to become a star maker, that's your next level of breakthrough. Until you can inspire someone else to be as good or better than you are at what you do, you're not a master. So you've got to make a decision. Do you want to be a star?"

Jim went on to tell me there was nothing wrong with choosing to be a star. Most people don't even make it to that level, and that I could continue on this path and become a trainer, and I would make a powerful difference in the world and get everything I wanted in life.

Two things happened immediately for me. First, I was completely clear about my next level of breakthrough and fully committed to it. I could see it and understand 100 percent what was coming. It was like a PING! in my body.

And second, I went into complete and total breakdown.

My inner Drift voice said, "I'm a failure, I'm a loser. I'm not good enough. I'm not worthy. Jim didn't mean all the nice things he said to compliment me; they were really a way to set me up so he could tell me that I sucked because I'd never coached or trained or developed anybody." In other words, my ego was triggered and inflamed, my buttons were pushed, and I went into a complete tailspin.

I had my pity party for about six hours that night, and, as soon as I got over my Drifty ego attack and let it go and the dust settled, I had a heart-to-heart talk with my authentic myself.

It went like this: What is this work truly about? Is this work about you, Michael? Is it about you being a star? Are you really going to get what you want? If it's all about you getting what you want, is that what this work is about? Do you need to be loved and adored? Why don't you be a rock star if that's what you want? Why don't you be an actor? Why don't you be a comic? (I had to pause here because I'm very funny.)

And clearly, I realized that I didn't want to be the center of attention. I wanted to be the center of intention.

I wanted to be the nucleus that sparks atoms of leadership throughout this world, throughout the galaxy, in every walk of life. In every community In our urban areas, in our cities, and in the ivory towers of the suburbs. From sea to shining sea.

I immediately changed my view of life and my role in it. AGAIN. This became the next level of breakthrough for me as a leader. My view now was this: I'm going to identify potential leadership stars, and I'm going to create stars in the work of transformation. I'm going to dedicate my life and my vision to transforming the world by creating a rippling effect of leadership, a rippling effect created by people that own the vision and possibility of transformation as if they thought of it themselves.

A PROGRAM FOR MASTER LEADERS

This is where my mastery of leadership program—which I now teach all over the world—was born. As a result of that conversation with Jim, I shifted my role, and I could see infinite possibilities to cause transformation faster and more efficiently.

Around the time of this conversation, I was promoted and became National Training Director. My new role was to coach and train our leadership trainers and area directors to stand as the source of transformation, as the source of their vision, to develop their ways of being and their skills so that they could become not only as good but ultimately, better than me.

In the early 1990s, I developed the concept of creating a mastery leadership program and the distinctions based on my research and my experience of master leaders throughout the world and throughout history.

Where did they operate from? What were their conversations? What were their interpretations? What were their attitudes? What were their beliefs? How did they show up in life? How do they show up in the world? What did they do? What did they cause, what were their results? What can I learn from them?

I developed a set of 12 distinctions, knowing that if I could— through the process of coaching and training—inspire students and other leaders to embrace them, to get them in their hearts, minds, and bodies, they would become an extension of me and more importantly, my leadership in the world. Not me, Michael. Not me, my personality. They would become an extension of the vision someone else inspired in me.

What I wanted to create within them was owning their vision for themselves and their vision of what's possible for the world, so they would go out professionally and personally in their sphere of influence and cause the most powerful impact and manifestation of that vision.

I knew that, together, we could ultimately shift The Drift.

STARS AND STAR MAKERS

That's the whole idea, of course. To shift The Drift, to create a critical mass where the people in the world are operating from like-minded distinctions, behaviors, ways of being and thoughts so that we create a domino effect that results in a win/win world for all.

The idea of critical mass is to have enough people enrolled in the conversations and distinctions and vision, and I mean enrolled as if they own it, as if they thought of it themselves. They are the author. And when they get to that space, bam! critical mass happens and the rest of the world is enrolled.

Change is happening. Shifts are occurring in The Drift. Progress is unfolding. We still have racism. We still have sexism, bigotry, prejudice, war, and terrorism. Clearly, we have work to do.

The "Times Up" and "Me Too" and "March for Our Lives" movements are ramping up conversations, marches, and peaceful yet powerful protests in ways that haven't been seen since the 1970s. They are led by vision-driven leaders who are creating other leaders.

We also have large pockets of people rising up into the vision, enrolled by a pioneer core group of critical-mass-thinking leaders committed to creating that global shift.

Transformation is happening on a "think globally, act locally" scale. I met Chris Hawker, who is now one of the co-founders of Next Level Trainings in Columbus, Ohio when he was a student participating in my mastery of leadership training.

Chris was there to become a trainer, to learn to be a master leader. By the time he completed the program, which is six months, his vision went from "I want to be a trainer; I want to do your job," to, "I want to open up a training center in Ohio. I want transformation to happen for the maximum number of people in the world and my community."

He enrolled me in believing he had what it takes to bring transformation to Ohio, and he enrolled me in wanting to support him in doing it. Talk about a flip. Chris went from "I want to be a star," to "I want to be a star-maker."

In this context, a star is a person who embodies the vision of what's possible for the world. These are master leaders who create such energy that when you're in their space, you feel it in your bones. They light you up, ignite something in you. You watch what they have, and you're not sure what it is, but you're attracted to it, like a beacon, like a guiding North Star. They invite you to immerse yourself in the highest possibility of life and living and stand as an example of what's possible when you live by vision.

The Drift's interpretation of a star is someone who is popular, famous; a celebrity who's great at what they do. But when I say star, I'm thinking of it through the eyes of transformation.

Everyone has different levels of mastery, including stars on the rise. Before I could ever be a star-maker in the work of leadership, I had to experience being a star.

The first level of breakthrough necessary on the journey to star is whatever holds someone back and stops them from embodying leadership at a master level. It might be responsibility, expert communication, operating by values, living the values that are consistent with vision, being committed to vision, or becoming a change master.

In other words, once you get the first 11 distinctions in your body, and I mean totally embrace and embody them consciously, you reach star level. When you get Distinction 12 and embody it, you too have the choice to move into star-maker, just like I did.

Being a star maker gives you the power, desire, knowledge, and expertise to be able to take somebody under your wing and bridge the gap between their leadership, their star potential, and their star-making potential.

Is everybody impassioned by that? No, not everybody is. Distinction 12 is the most challenging part of mastering leadership. You may remember the story I referenced in the chapter on Distinction 5 about Magic Johnson quitting as coach of the Los Angeles Lakers after just three weeks. I believe Magic struggled to go from star to star-maker.

He didn't have the ability or the vision to use his knowledge, wisdom, talents, and skills and share them with the people he was coaching. He was unable to impart leadership in such a way that they were inspired to be as good or better than he was. Does that take anything away from Magic Johnson as a player? No. Does it take anything away from his NBA Hall of Fame career and place in the Top 10 greatest players of all time? No, it doesn't take anything away from Magic, but it does show how challenging it can be to be a star maker.

My leadership mastery program has been taught in the United States, South America, and Europe throughout the last 20 years, and I estimate 4,000 students have graduated. Of those 4,000 students, I would say 25 percent have reached the level of star in the work of transformation, have become someone who really embodies the vision, is committed to the vision, lives the vision, and owns the vision.

If I called a global transformational leadership meeting with a light in the sky like the bat signal, I would bet my life at least one in four of the students would show up for the meeting, along with the star-makers.

Out of the 1,000 or so leadership students that are now stars, I'd estimate that 100 are star makers, including my partner and friend Chris Lee. Some of the leaders quoted in this book—Chris Hawker, Brad Ballard, and Jenna Phillips Ballard—are on the path.

The idea of creating leadership in others is the art of sharing and giving generously. It is taking the work of leadership and transformation professionally or personally to the next level by committing to full partnership in it, one hundred percent.

BUSINESS LEADERS CREATE OTHER BUSINESS LEADERS

Stars and star-makers exist at every level and every place in society. Master leaders create stars at work and stars in their families; there is no limit to the ways leaders create other leaders.

Take Apple, for example. If Apple's success belonged to Steve Jobs alone, then when he died, what would have happened to Apple? Apple is worth more now under the leadership of Tim Cook than it was when Steve Jobs was at the helm. The company has continued to grow, is still producing new and fresh products, and its profitability is higher. The sign of a healthy organization is that its success doesn't hinge upon a person or their personality. It's been estimated that Apple could be worth one trillion dollars.

For contrast, the Trump organization is losing money during Trump's presidency. I would assert this is because his organization was driven by his personality. Without his focus, the organization is less successful.

Natalie Jill is an uber-successful brand in the fitness world. Its founder, Natalie Jill, recently completed my Mastery Leadership Program (MLP) at Ascension Leadership Academy (ALA) in San Diego. She's created huge success in her business. She's already a star in her work and her field. So why did she enroll in my course? Because she's committed to developing herself as a master leader.

Natalie Jill is not a star in the work of transformation. She promotes herself and her business through social media, and with presentations to mass audiences. That's a different experience than working with an audience in person, which is where transformational training happens. For some people, talking into a camera is much easier than leading a workshop or seminar for a live audience. That's a much bigger stretch for her because it requires her to be vulnerable, visible, and intimate in an uncomfortable space.

Natalie also wants to be a star maker in her organization; she wants the people in her company to own the vision. She wants to create around her a high level of leadership and partnership and ownership from her key people, so she can trust them, count on them, rely on them. That highest level of leadership, vision, and partnership allows her to take a vacation, to have the time, space, and energy to focus on other projects and develop other business ideas.

It's hard to focus on the vision if you're constantly plugging holes in the ship and focused on keeping it afloat.

"Being an entrepreneur and having strong visions, it's frustrating to feel like I'm tasking other people constantly, and that I have a lot of people just waiting for me to give them a task," Natalie says. "I've learned through Michael's training how to enroll others in my vision, so they can lead and make decisions and create solutions vs. it always being me."

"I impact lots of people and help them break through their self-imposed stops. Most people come to me for fat loss. They think it's nutrition and fitness, but really it's a lot of self-imposed stories that they've told themselves, and it holds them back from becoming their best selves. I tell people I kill fat for a living, but it's really more than that. It's also killing a false truth that people carry. That's a different kind of fat, and I help them break through it."

Master leaders hire other leaders. The most successful organizations bring people in with an upward mobility strategy.

When I am hiring people to work with me in my organization, I'm not looking for an assistant who will stay an assistant. When I hire someone, I'm hiring them from a vision of what's possible. I'm hiring for the position that I'm currently committed to filling and a minimum of two promotions down the road. In the context of leaders hiring other leaders, someone may start as a janitor and end up as office manager. Or start as office manager, but end up as a sales rep. Or begin as VP of sales and end up as CEO of the company. If I cannot see someone at that next level, if I cannot see them thriving in the organization down the road, I don't hire them.

That's the way master leaders think--creating leadership in others, holding people in their highest possibility and engaging only in conversations, beliefs, attitudes, and behaviors that lead to those possibilities becoming real.

Championship teams are built the same way. Being in business can often feel like a constant 911 emergency, even when it really isn't. Leaders who produce the same breakdowns over and over again often make decisions out of stress, fear, desperation, laziness, and hope. None of these strategies will create excellence and success. Just ask yourself, what would Abigail Johnson do? Theo Epstein? Mary Barra? Michael Rapino? Daymond John? If you don't know who these extraordinary leaders are, I suggest you look them up as soon as you finish this chapter.

MASTER LEADERS CHOOSE LEADERSHIP

No matter who you are, what you do for a living, where you live, how much money you have, and who your friends are, you can either choose survival in The Drift, or you can choose leadership. You CAN become a master leader—someone who is vision-driven, who dedicates, studies, and embodies the 12 Distinctions of Leadership.

In reality, choosing to live in The Drift is easier than choosing to lead. From the perspective of The Drift, the world is a place of chaos and distrust and apathy and pain. It's not safe, so we hide in our comfort zones and lock our doors.

"It's easy to get lost, scared, contract and curl up into a ball and forget," says my friend and colleague Dr. Judith Rich, who is a 44-year veteran in the work of transformation. "I think that's why transformational leaders (and in my mind that's potentially everyone and anyone) are so critical now. It's so important to stand in the midst of this and remind people of the context that we're operating in and continuously hold that vision and encourage people to keep standing, to continue to awaken others. I truly believe that that's our job. And that's why I, at age 76, still have passion and energy for this vision. It's still very much alive and awake in me."

Master leaders choose leadership. Over and over. In every moment. The work of transformation is not easy work in the beginning. For those who truly embrace it, who embody and live it, it eventually becomes a part of their DNA, and it becomes who they are, not what they do.

Jenna Phillips Ballard is a transformational trainer and the co-founder of ALA in San Diego. Jenna is a master leader.

"I've always said that leaders are not meant to fit in, and that's what The Drift is, fitting in. To choose leadership is really a huge responsibility and it's also a really powerful choice. When somebody truly wants to be a leader, what they get to create and choose into every single day is being willing to do what's not popular, be willing to stand out, be willing to be judged or criticized."

A very small percentage of people in the world actually do choose leadership, and of that percentage, an even smaller percentage of people choose to be responsible and integrous leaders. What's available for every single person who is on this path to leadership is that we get to continue to be students of life, for life. I don't believe in being done with our learning experience. We're either green and growing or ripe and rotting in The Drift."

The truest test of your ability to master leadership is your ability to create leadership in others. Isn't it the dream of every parent to have their children have a better life than their own? To avoid making the same mistakes or suffer from the decisions we've made? To learn from our vast lessons and experience? I believe it's in the essence of who we are to lead. To make the world a better and brighter place than the one we've found and lived in.

The opportunity here and now is to commit yourself to find, discover, and step into your vision and purpose in life. To declare a purpose that demands the best of yourself, your higher self. To dedicate yourself to giving the vision away to the maximum number of people.

Each of us is writing our own epitaph, right now, while we are alive. It's a myth that it happens after we're gone. Make it matter that you were here. Give your gifts away with urgency and abundance.

With each of us accessing our visions—led by the 12 Distinctions of Master Leaders—our world will never be the same. Together, we'll continue to shift The Drift.

**CREATING OTHER LEADERS:
LIGHTING THE INTERNAL
FLAME**

What will it take for you to become a leadership star? A star-maker?

_____

_____

_____

_____

_____

_____

_____

_____

_____

What's possible for you to create when you ignite the fire of leadership in others?

_____

_____

_____

_____

_____

_____

_____

_____

_____

What's possible for you when you live the 12 Distinctions of Master Leaders? Which is your biggest challenge? Which will make the most difference for you professionally and personally?

_____

_____

_____

_____

_____

_____

_____

_____

_____

_____

_____

Write your own epitaph, having lived the life of your vision.

_____

_____

_____

_____

_____

_____

_____

_____

_____

_____

RESOURCES

Ascension Leadership Academy
San Diego, CA
https://alasandiego.com/

Energia Positiva
Netherlands and Spain
http://www.energiapositivanederland.nl/
http://www.energiapositiva.es/

Espacio Vital Global
Phoenix, AZ and El Paso, TX
https://www.espaciovitalg.com/

Impacto Vital
Mexico City, Mexico
http://www.mexicoimpactovital.com/

Impacto Vital
San Juan, Puerto Rico
http://impactovitalpr.co/

Mastery in Transformational Training
Culver City, CA
https://www.mittraining.com/

Next Level Trainings
Columbus, OH and Philadelphia, PA
https://www.nextleveltrainings.com/

Heartcore Business
Solana Beach, CA
http://www.heartcorebusiness.com/

INDEX

INDEX